WHO'S MINDING THE MONEY?

An Investment Guide for Nonprofit Board Members
SECOND EDITION

Robert P. Fry, Jr.

BOARDSOURCE®
Building Effective Nonprofit Boards

Library of Congress Cataloging-in-Publication Data

Fry, Robert P.

Who's minding the money? : an investment guide for nonprofit board members / by Robert P. Fry, Jr.

    p. cm. --

ISBN 1-58686-113-1

1. Nonprofit organizations--Finance.
2. Nonprofit organizations--Management.
3. Investments. I. Title.

          HG4027.65.F79 2009
          658.15'6--dc22   2009015806

BoardSource was established in 1988 by the Association of Governing Boards of Universities and Colleges (AGB) and Independent Sector (IS). Prior to this, in the early 1980s, the two organizations had conducted a survey and found that although 30 percent of respondents believed they were doing a good job of board education and training, the rest of the respondents reported little, if any, activity in strengthening governance. As a result, AGB and IS proposed the creation of a new organization whose mission would be to increase the effectiveness of nonprofit boards.

With a lead grant from the Kellogg Foundation and funding from five other donors, BoardSource opened its doors in 1988 as the National Center for Nonprofit Boards with a staff of three and an operating budget of $385,000. On January 1, 2002, BoardSource took on its new name and identity. These changes were the culmination of an extensive process of understanding how we were perceived, what our audiences wanted, and how we could best meet the needs of nonprofit organizations.

Today BoardSource is the premier voice of nonprofit governance. Its highly acclaimed products, programs, and services mobilize boards so that organizations fulfill their missions, achieve their goals, increase their impact, and extend their influence. BoardSource is a 501(c)(3) organization.

BoardSource provides

- resources to nonprofit leaders through workshops, training, and an extensive Web site (www.boardsource.org)

- governance consultants who work directly with nonprofit leaders to design specialized solutions to meet an organization's needs

- the world's largest, most comprehensive selection of material on nonprofit governance, including a large selection of books and CD-ROMs

- an annual conference that brings together approximately 900 governance experts, board members, and chief executives and senior staff from around the world

For more information, please visit our Web site at www.boardsource.org, e-mail us at mail@boardsource.org, or call us at 800-883-6262.

Have You Used These BoardSource Resources?

THE GOVERNANCE SERIES

1. *Ten Basic Responsibilities of Nonprofit Boards, Second Edition*
2. *Legal Responsibilities of Nonprofit Boards, Second Edition*
3. *Financial Responsibilities of Nonprofit Boards, Second Edition*
4. *Fundraising Responsibilities of Nonprofit Boards, Second Edition*
5. *The Nonprofit Board's Role in Mission, Planning, and Evaluation, Second Edition*
6. *Structures and Practices of Nonprofit Boards, Second Edition*

BOOKS

Understanding Nonprofit Financial Statements, Third Edition

The Nonprofit Dashboard: A Tool for Tracking Progress

Navigating the Organizational Lifecycle: A Capacity-Building Guide for Nonprofit Leaders

Financial Committees

The Nonprofit Legal Landscape

The Nonprofit Board's Guide to Bylaws

Managing Conflicts of Interest: A Primer for Nonprofit Boards, Second Edition

The Nonprofit Policy Sampler, Second Edition

Chief Executive Transitions: How to Hire and Support a Nonprofit CEO

Chief Executive Succession Planning: The Board's Role in Securing Your Organization's Future

Assessment of the Chief Executive

The Board Chair Handbook, Second Edition

Getting the Best from Your Board: An Executive's Guide to a Successful Partnership

Moving Beyond Founder's Syndrome to Nonprofit Success

The Source: Twelve Principles of Governance That Power Exceptional Boards

Exceptional Board Practices: The Source in Action

Fearless Fundraising for Nonprofit Boards, Second Edition

Driving Strategic Planning: A Nonprofit Executive's Guide

Taming the Troublesome Board Member

Meet Smarter: A Guide to Better Nonprofit Board Meetings

The Nonprofit Board Answer Book: A Practical Guide for Board Members and Chief Executives, Second Edition

The Board Building Cycle: Nine Steps to Finding, Recruiting, and Engaging Nonprofit Board Members, Second Edition

Culture of Inquiry: Healthy Debate in the Boardroom

DVDs

Meeting the Challenge: An Orientation to Nonprofit Board Service

Speaking of Money: A Guide to Fundraising for Nonprofit Board Members

For an up-to-date list of publications and information about current prices, membership, and other services, please call BoardSource at 800-883-6262 or visit our Web site at www.boardsource.org.

CONTENTS

PREFACE **1**
What You'll Find in This Book 2

INTRODUCTION **3**
Who's in Charge? 3
Why Invest? 4

CHAPTER 1 *The Basics* **7**
Identifying Assets to Be Managed 8
Identifying Investment Goals, Time Frames, and Restrictions 8
Assessing Tolerance for Risk 11
How Do We Recognize Risk? 13
Creating Helpful Policies and Structures 15
Conculsion 16

CHAPTER 2 *Investment Concepts for Board Members* **19**
Total Return 20
The Importance of Time in Managing Money 21
Performance Reporting as an Investment Management Tool 23
Portfolio Theory to Control Risk 25
Modern Portfolio Theory vs. Reality 28

CHAPTER 3 *The Legal Environment* **33**
Background: The Prudent Man Rule 33
The Prudent Investor Rule Today 35
Costs of Investment Management 39
Fund Pooling 40
Limits of the Uniform Acts 40
The Constraint of Broader Fiduciary Duty 42

CHAPTER 4 *Unique Issues Facing Nonprofits* **43**
The Role of an Investment Committee 43
Source and Character of Funds 45
Interaction between Investment Policy and Donors 46
Socially-Responsible Investing 48
Scam-Proofing 51
Spending Policy 52
Conflicts of Interest 56

CHAPTER 5 *Getting Help* **61**
Investment Tasks and Service Providers 61
Passive Structures vs. Active Advisors 63
The Importance and Role of a Consultant 65

CHAPTER 6 *21st Century Investment Issues* **67**
Globalization 67
Alternative Investments 68
The Dangers of Fiat Currencies 74

CONCLUSION **77**
What to Do When the Wheels Fall Off the Bus 77
Look Hopefully to the Future 78

APPENDIX I *Sample Investment Policies* **79**

APPENDIX II *Alternative Investment Due Diligence Guidelines* **85**

APPENDIX III *Sample Spending Policy* **89**

APPENDIX IV *Uniform Prudent Management of Institutional Funds Act* **91**

APPENDIX V *Self-Guided Investment Audit* **99**

GLOSSARY **115**

SUGGESTED RESOURCES **121**

ACKNOWLEDGMENTS **127**

ABOUT THE AUTHOR **129**

PREFACE

The five years since the publication of the first edition of this book (then called *Minding the Money)* have been among the most turbulent in U.S. investment history. Stock markets both at home and abroad have been through exhilarating highs and staggering lows. Given this recent history, only a fool would approach investing with an easy confidence that he knows exactly what he is doing.

The good news is that if we can honestly face our lack of understanding with even a modest admission of ignorance — perhaps by admitting we did not expect global stock markets to lose half their value in 18 months — then there is hope of doing a much better job going forward. Humility is a powerful investment management tool.

Unfortunately, humility is more often preached than practiced, especially in the business world. Humble people are often at a disadvantage when trying to sell their services, and this sad truth applies to investment managers as much as anyone else. However, when markets lose trillions of dollars in a single year, largely through professionally managed funds of one sort or another, it is at least fair to wonder if the managers' self-confidence is misplaced.

With that in mind, I have tried to model some humility in updating this book by including a number of Practical Observations. In these Observations, I share real-world examples of implementing the policies the book recommends, and in some cases I admit my own fallibility. By including these stories, I hope to make it a little easier for all of us to wrestle with the investment world in which we now live.

Closely related to humility is transparency about what people in the investment industry actually do, and how they are compensated. All of us tend to skew our advice toward activities for which we are paid. Even as I look back on earlier editions of this book, I see the occasional place where my work at that time colored my advice. To anticipate my prejudices, the reader should understand that I work as an investment management consultant to institutional investors. My consulting role is the lens through which I see the investment world.

As consultants, we advise clients on overall investment strategy, which ultimately takes the form of an asset allocation model for each portfolio or fund. In addition, we then search for appropriate managers, mutual funds, hedge funds, and other instruments through which to implement the recommended allocations. Finally, we regularly report on the resulting investment performance.

In addition, we work very closely with the officers and directors of our largest client, the National Christian Foundation (NCF). For them, we are effectively an outsourced Chief Investment Officer, doing everything from pure, institutional-style consulting to advising on daily corporate cash management. In that arena, my daily work life is more like that of an inside officer than that of an outside consultant. I meet at least twice per year with the investment committee of the board of directors and every month with the internal investment management team. In addition, I speak a couple of times a day with NCF's Chief Financial Officer and/or other members of his team by phone, e-mail or text message.

Since the publication of the first edition of this book, I also wrote a more extensive book on the same subject: *Nonprofit Investment Policies: Practical Steps for Growing Charitable Funds*. The publisher, John Wiley & Sons, has graciously allowed me to excerpt passages from that book in this one. Those of you wishing to read more detailed discussions of the concepts presented here may find the longer book useful.

WHAT YOU'LL FIND IN THIS BOOK

This book contains information intended to help all those who assist not-for-profit organizations with the investment of their funds. The material includes a discussion of portfolio theory as well as an overview of the relevant legal environment. It also covers hiring advisors and monitoring their performance. Along the way, there is advice on appropriate board and committee structures as they relate to investing an organization's funds. The book concludes with a discussion of current investment issues. The appendices include a sample set of policies, a copy of applicable laws, a sample self-guided investment audit, and some alternative investment due diligence guidelines. Also the attached CD-ROM includes customizable versions of each appendix.

INTRODUCTION

This book is a guide to key investment management issues for anyone involved in managing the financial assets of a nonprofit organization. Because of the central role and key responsibilities of the governing board, we will often discuss matters from the perspective of a trustee or director. However, what we say should be equally valuable help to corporate officers, employees, outside advisors, and even key volunteers. Throughout, we will emphasize those aspects of investment management that tend to be unique or of particular importance in the nonprofit world.

In that regard, we assume that the reader understands basic investment concepts apart from the nonprofit context. Thus, we will not review the definitions of stocks and bonds; the operation of the markets; the normal business functions of banks, brokers, and other advisors; or the fundamentals of corporate finance. (There are already a great many books on the market that cover these topics. For readers who want an enjoyable discussion of investment basics, my personal favorite is *A Random Walk Down Wall Street,* by Burton Malkiel, first published in 1973 and now in its ninth edition. For other useful references, see the list of Suggested Resources at the end of the book.)

WHO'S IN CHARGE?

In the nonprofit world, the answer to the question "Who's in charge?" is not always obvious. As in the for-profit world, executives frequently think and act as if they were in complete control. Often, in fact, they are — because the board has taken no interest in investment decisions. Sometimes major donors believe they are in charge, by virtue of the organization's dependence on their financial support. Even when such donors have no legal authority over the organization's funds, they may still exercise a great deal of *de facto* control. Finally, there is the occasional nonprofit that is controlled by one or more third parties. The community foundations run by various commercial investment firms, such as Fidelity or Vanguard, are examples of this model.

In virtually every case, however, *legal* responsibility for supervising investments resides squarely with the board of directors. Whatever authority other parties may have to influence or implement investment decisions, such authority ought to be shaped, guided, and constrained by the oversight of an informed board, following well-designed policies and procedures. The alternative, as we will see in later chapters, can be a legal nightmare in which the board members incur personal liability for the actions of people they have not effectively supervised.

The fundamental challenge for board members is to balance their legal responsibilities against the organization's practical needs. The executive staff is almost always responsible for daily operations, with the CEO or (more commonly) the CFO handling investment operations, including the supervision of outside service providers. But as much as the board needs the executive team's service, the board may not abdicate its responsibility to supervise. Good policies help maintain the right balance. With effective policies and procedures, a board can be very active in supervising investments while still delegating authority, encouraging teamwork and community spirit, and articulating a common vision. To do all this, however, board members also need a working knowledge of the key features of their investment environment.

We'll begin addressing the knowledge requirement in Chapter One. In the meantime, for board members there's a short answer to the question of who's in charge. You are. Who's minding the money? You are. The goal of this book is to help you do the job enjoyably and well.

PRACTICAL OBSERVATION 1
YOU CAN'T JUST "FIRE AND FORGET"

The single most difficult aspect of supervising investments, at least for me, is that you can never take your eyes off the target. What I would really like, truth be told, is for investment management to be just like a Sidewinder missile. This heat-seeking missile, once fired, tracks the target aircraft automatically. The pilot can fire and forget, or fire and turn hard toward home — things I have often wanted to do as an investor.

The reality, cruelly driven home in the last couple of years, is that investing, and supervising those who invest, requires ongoing diligence, ongoing involvement and ongoing review. There are no Sidewinder investment formulas. Recognizing that fact, however, makes the task of investing the right way a little easier. Everything in this book is intended to provide a rudimentary framework within which to conduct ongoing supervision. Don't expect your investment missiles to hit their targets if you aren't providing regular guidance.

WHY INVEST?

Since investing seems fraught with all kinds of problems, before we talk about how to do it correctly we should address a more fundamental question: Why invest at all? The answer has several parts: the need to offset inflation, the value of a reduced need for fundraising, and (most fundamentally) the imperative of good stewardship.

INFLATION

The insidiousness of inflation is that it erodes the value of cash. If one holds currency or cash equivalents during a period in which there is any inflation at all, the purchasing power, and therefore the true value, of the assets declines. In a noninflationary environment, the failure to earn adequate interest results in lost opportunities but not true economic losses. Money in the bank at 2 percent interest generates a real return of 2 percent. But adding inflation to the mix can be lethal: A mere 3 percent inflation rate means that 2 percent annual interest paid on a bank account means a true economic loss of 1 percent per year. Even in a very low-inflation economy, if your organization is not able to "out-earn" inflation, you are effectively allowing funds to waste away over time. Inflation, then, compels an organization to invest as a means of caring for and preserving the value of its assets.

OPPORTUNITIES FOR GROWTH

An additional reason to invest assets is to exploit the growth potential such funds represent. Accumulated funds with a longer time horizon represent an opportunity to increase revenues by investing for higher anticipated returns. An extra few percentage points of total return can, over the years, make an enormous difference in the financial health and asset base of an organization.

Additional investment income can be of even greater benefit to organizations whose principal support requires active fundraising. The true cost of fundraising in the nonprofit world tends to be understated. No matter how accurate the accounting of fundraising expenses, that accounting rarely (if ever) captures the "lost opportunity" costs in time, effort, and energy that fundraising exacts from staff, executives, and board members. Additional funds from investment returns can ease these pressures.

GOOD STEWARDSHIP

Whenever other people entrust their assets to you for a charitable purpose, you assume an obligation to handle those funds responsibly. Of course that means trying to grow the money without losing it. But more fundamentally: Investing is *unavoidable*. Any surplus, even cash in a non–interest-bearing checking account, is invested. The organization, as the owner of the funds, is allowing another institution — a bank — to hold those funds in exchange for a return, which in this case is the providing of checking services. While that might not be a *good* investment, since the organization can probably get both checking services *and* interest on its funds, it is nonetheless an investment. Once we understand this, we realize that "Why invest?" is not exactly the right question to ask. The real question, if we want to be good stewards, is "How do we invest well?"

At the end of the day, the payoff for good stewardship is not measured merely in dollars. Nonprofits typically invite others to join their cause or mission by supporting the organization with gifts of time, talent, or treasure. Employees who work for nonprofits often make a significant personal contribution by choosing a lower-paying career track. One of the ways a nonprofit compensates its supporters for their sacrifices is by giving them the joy of being involved with an organization worthy of their support. The existence of well-managed funds, and the public commitment to good management through published policies and procedures, can heighten both the perceived and the actual worthiness of the entire organization. Among other things, it can help allay fears of the future by implying, "We plan to be here for the long haul." Doing a good job with the money is simply part of all we do as nonprofits to encourage and honor the commitments we ask of others.

PRACTICAL OBSERVATION 2
THERE'S NO SUCH THING AS A FREE-INTEREST LUNCH

In the first edition of this book, I strongly hinted that holding funds in a non–interest-bearing checking account was a poor investment. That sentiment was informed by a number of assumptions, some of which were proven wrong by the credit crisis that began in the summer of 2007. For one thing, I tacitly assumed that money market mutual funds offered by or through major brokerage firms were, practically speaking, just as safe as checking accounts at federally insured banks. It followed that if you could earn greater interest by using a money market fund in conjunction with a commercial checking account, that was obviously the right thing to do.

The assumption proved fallible. In September of 2008, following the bankruptcy of Lehman Brothers, the Reserve Primary Fund (a large, well-established money market fund) announced that it had "broken the buck," shortly after which it froze investor redemptions. Investors in the fund, who probably thought of it as a substitute for cash in the bank, could no longer get at their money. For anyone with bills to pay, lack of access to one's funds can be almost as devastating as actual losses.

It is easy enough to see why investors in the Reserve Primary Fund were confident of its safety. This was the first money market mutual fund in the United States and, at more than $60 billion just prior to its collapse, one of the largest. The resulting rush of investors trying to withdraw their money from this and other money market funds was so potentially damaging to the entire financial system that on September 19, 2008, the U.S.Federal Reserve used emergency powers to guarantee all institutional and retail money market funds whose sponsors chose to participate in the program. Virtually all fund sponsors accepted the offer.

One practical lesson of this episode is that even extremely safe investments require constant monitoring. In short, we have to approach decisions about where to deposit our cash with the same level of scrutiny and due diligence we would apply to hiring an investment manager, picking a stock, or investing in a hedge fund. Risk is everywhere.

CHAPTER 1
THE BASICS

A number of years ago, I wrote that "the investment environment today is innovative, accessible, and overwhelmingly friendly to the success of charitable participants," as a result of which "there is no longer any reason for a charitable organization of any size to fail to participate in the securities market in a measured and disciplined way."[1]

While that statement may seem odd in light of the investment carnage of recent years, it was true then — and it is true today. The investment world is wide open, in the sense that an organization with even a small amount of funds can participate right alongside the more richly endowed ones on a fairly level playing field. The advantages held by the big investors, the insiders, and the powers of the industry, while real, nonetheless pale in comparison to the value of good judgment and a steady hand.

This is not to minimize the enormous problems on Wall Street, as evidenced by the near-destruction of the major U.S. banks during the credit crisis. Nor will I deny the existence of unscrupulous and sometimes fraudulent behavior. But these problems tend to affect the well-connected and the uninformed more or less equally. Remember that the overwhelming majority of the funds in the markets are managed by full-time professionals, through mutual funds, hedge funds, and institutional accounts. When under that arrangement the markets lose trillions of dollars in a single year (that's trillions, with a "T"), the presumed advantages of the industry insiders appear less impressive. Professional advisors really do have something to offer, as we discuss at some length in Chapter 5. But the active involvement of "normal people" — directors, officers, and other employees — is vital.

So, investing is truly an equal-opportunity venture, but it is never easy. Rather, investing is an inherently risky enterprise in which your willingness to take a risk is part of why others pay you a return for the use of your money.

Besides being risky, investing can also be confusing — a world with too many choices that, at times, all sound the same. So before dealing with fiduciary and nonprofit investment issues, we will look at the preliminary questions governing boards should ask themselves:

- What assets are available to be managed?

- What are our investment goals, time frames, and restrictions?

---

[1] Fry, Robert P., Jr. *Nonprofit Investment Policies: Practical Steps for Growing Charitable Funds.* Hoboken, NJ: John Wiley & Sons, 1998.

- What is our tolerance for risk?

- How do we recognize risk?

- What structures and policies need to be created to reach our goals?

While the boardroom is the appropriate venue to discuss and decide these questions, the board members do not need to do all, or even most, of the actual work. As is normal in a corporate structure, board members may rely upon both executive staff and outside advisors. But in each of these areas, board members must make the critical decisions and, together with the chief executive, set the tone for the investment environment. Such leadership is uniquely a board function.

IDENTIFYING ASSETS TO BE MANAGED

Frequently, nonprofit organizations own or control far more in the way of financial assets than their leaders realize. In part this is because assets may exist in different places and forms. Some of the more common categories of investable assets include

- operating reserves

- retirement funds

- capital campaign reserves

- endowments

- planned gift assets (gift annuity reserves, trusts, pooled-income funds)

Each of these sources or categories of funds will usually have unique investment time horizons, risk tolerance and return requirements, liquidity needs and, in some cases, tax characteristics or other restrictions. Consequently, the first of the basics of nonprofit investment management is to identify the sources and character of an organization's funds. Appendix V provides a self-assessment tool to help identify and categorize a nonprofit organization's investment assets.

IDENTIFYING INVESTMENT GOALS, TIME FRAMES, AND RESTRICTIONS

To make investment decisions, an organization must assess the context within which the decisions are to be made. In the investment world, that context includes

- the time frames available

- the investment goals (e.g., growth, current income, or preservation of capital)

- any specific restrictions or limitations on the organization or the funds in question

Goals and time frames are commonly identified at the fund level. With operating reserves, for example, typical objectives would be to preserve capital, maintain complete liquidity, and earn whatever level of interest is possible without violating the first two objectives. Since the operating-reserve time frame is usually "right now," the goals for these funds will generally dictate investment in a checking account, money market fund, or other comparable instrument.

Normally, the organization's cash flow requirements will guide the determination of how much money constitutes a reasonable operating reserve. That amount might be expressed as a cash minimum, a percentage of the annual budget, or an amount sufficient to operate for a stated time period. I'm not aware of any universally adopted formula. It is clear, however, that organizations with large fluctuations in cash flow or receivables usually need larger operating reserves than organizations with steady income.

At the other end of the spectrum, the goal for an organization's endowment funds would likely be to increase the fund as much as possible in anticipation of future spending. In that case, the time frame is essentially open-ended and the current spending requirement is typically both limited and very predictable. Given those criteria, the funds can be invested as aggressively as the risk tolerance of the board (discussed below) will allow.

Capital campaign funds fall somewhere in the middle. They often represent monies for which growth would be fine but is not essential, and for which there is no current spending requirement. However, the entire sum will probably be spent at or by a specific point in time, and so a portfolio of medium-term, fixed-income investments is probably most suitable. (However, note the giant caveat on bond risks in Practical Observation 3.)

There may also be restrictions that apply on an organization-wide basis. Socially- or morally-based investment criteria, the tax character of an organization (such as a private foundation), or specific legal restrictions on the investments that certain organizations are allowed to make — these are all examples of rules that would restrict the investment of organizational funds. In later chapters on the legal environment, portfolio theory, and unique issues facing nonprofits, I will discuss such restrictions and identify methods for addressing them.

PRACTICAL OBSERVATION 3
SOMETIMES LESS IS MORE — PARTICULARLY IN THE WORLD OF BONDS

Jim Grant, a well-known Wall Street skeptic and the editor of *Grant's Interest Rate Observer,* once referred to corporate bonds as "return-free risk." The point is well taken. Bonds are loans, nothing less — but, also, importantly, nothing more. That is to say, pretty much all bonds offer limited return: If everything goes well, you get your money back with interest. But even this limited return comes at some risk.

In fact, bonds may not be significantly safer than other, more obviously risky investments. The problem is that bond risks are not as well understood as the risks associated with stocks. There are at least three bond risks that really matter. The first is principal risk due to the default of the issuer. If the issuer is any entity other than the U.S. government, then there is a risk of default. Corporate failures in recent years, such as the bankruptcy of Lehman Brothers, have made this risk more apparent.

Second, there is interest rate risk. Bonds, once issued, trade on markets at values that reflect the amount they pay in interest and the length of time to maturity. If available interest rates rise, then older, outstanding bonds with lower interest payments drop in value on the market. The longer money is tied up, the greater this risk becomes. A 2 or 3 percent rise in the general level of interest rates can lead to a 20 percent or 30 percent drop in the market value of long-term bonds. If it turns out that you need to spend the entire amount of your bond portfolio at that time, you are toast.*

The third important bond risk is inflation. Assume, for example, that you hold a 4-percent, 20-year U.S. Treasury bond. In terms of principal or default risk, such bonds are considered risk-free. And that may be a fair assumption, as the consequences of a U.S. government default would be catastrophic. But what if instead of defaulting, the government expands the money supply in a way that leads to massive inflation? In that event, interest rates will rise, decreasing your bond's market value as just described. In addition, the value of the eventual principal payment will erode by the cumulative amount of inflation over the life of the bond. Figuratively speaking, you may end up lending dollars and receiving back dimes.

So what is the right attitude toward bonds? In my professional practice, when the circumstances require investments in bonds, we have stayed very short-term (which almost always means three to five years or less), and we have leaned heavily toward U.S. government debt. We rarely seek the incrementally greater yields that are often available from corporate debt. There are, of course, many investment managers who would disagree with this philosophy and routinely invest in corporate bonds. And in fairness, there have been many times when our caution has left money on the table. But in this arena we prefer to take our incremental return in the form of the peace of mind that our very cautious approach to bonds provides.

* I apologize for using technical language. "Toast" is the term we sophisticated investment professionals use to describe our clients' condition when we have given them bad advice.

ASSESSING TOLERANCE FOR RISK

Perhaps the most important determination any board must make is the acceptable level of risk for each type of fund being invested. A board must make this "gut call" and must be comfortable with it. Otherwise, losses may cause board members to panic and demand investment strategy changes that disrupt well-laid plans and force hasty, unwise choices.

How should the decision be made? It requires a thoughtful and frank discussion by board members with input from investment advisors and executive staff. I like to start with a simple question: How much of a loss can we tolerate in this fund over the next one or two years without feeling compelled to change our investment strategy? It is important that the answer be expressed not just in percentage terms, but also in hard dollars. I occasionally hear a board member say something like "I could accept a 20 percent drop in our $5 million endowment over the next two years." But when I have tried to confirm this by restating the loss in dollar terms — "So you'd be ready to see the endowment decline by $1 million?" — the reaction has often been "No!" If you are a board member, you probably can and will translate your risk-tolerance back into percentage terms for management purposes. Still, thinking of the actual dollars involved is a clarifying exercise.

Risk tolerance will, and should, vary from fund to fund. A professional advisor may use additional questions, such as those found in Part IV of Appendix V, to aid board members in their thinking. But in the end, it is vital that a board clearly inform its advisors and executive staff of the risk it is willing to accept for each fund. Remember the bottom line: **Some things cannot be delegated. Only the board can set investment goals and determine its own appetite for risk.** Once risk levels are established, the board's professional advisor can forecast relative risks for the board members and can quantify the likelihood of adverse results. These are not guarantees, of course, only guidance.

The risk-assessment process should be iterative. Having once assessed risk tolerance for an organization or for a particular fund, **the board** (or investment committee) **should periodically** (at least annually) **review the assumptions on which risk-tolerance decisions were made.** It may seem odd that tolerance for risk would change, but in fact it does. Greater experience, improvement in overall financial strength, or changes in board membership may lead to an increase in risk tolerance. Conversely, an extended period of poor investment performance or an unanticipated need for immediate spending may provoke a decision to reduce risk exposure.

PRACTICAL OBSERVATION 4
WHAT RISKS ARE WE ALREADY TAKING?

Assessment of risk tolerance has to be realistic. For an investment advisor, it is frustrating to have to defend a "risky recommendation" against the objections of a group of people unaware of the risks they have tacitly accepted already. In uncertain times, it is perhaps reasonable for a director to ask the investment advisor, "Why should we invest any money in the stock market?" But this kind of question often hints at a false assumption that the current investment position is risk-free. There may well be incremental risks, or greater volatility risks, or risks of a different character, in taking the money from wherever it is and investing it in stocks. But the current allocation, whatever it is, is not risk-free.

To illustrate: Earlier in this chapter I recommended a high-liquidity allocation, like a checking account, for funds with a short time frame. But in addition to the risk of gradual value erosion due to inflation (see Practical Observation 1 in the Introduction), there is the risk of abrupt, catastrophic loss, due to bank failure, of uninsured deposits. A large organization may, on any given day, have $5 million or more on deposit with the bank. Since only the first $100,000 is FDIC insured,* the organization has essentially made a $4.9 million investment in a single, highly leveraged entity. And these entities do fail, even in the best of times. This is an issue of particular concern to larger organizations. As simple and nonspeculative as a checking account might seem, the allocation involves, unfortunately, a non-zero degree of risk. If the bank fails, large depositors convert their cash accounts to claims in a bankruptcy court.

The essence of this practical observation is twofold. First, the digging recommended in the next section is important and needs to be ongoing. It is easy to be lulled into a false sense of security by good service or the absence of bad news. Second, all risk conversations need to be contextual. The real question is, "How much *extra* risk are we going to take with any given action or investment... and is the anticipated reward worth it?" It is impossible to overstate the need for this mindset, or its countercultural character. I do not recall any director or chief financial officer ever saying to me, "Our money is *invested* in our checking account." No one thinks of money in the bank as an investment, and therefore everyone assumes it is safe. That is a false, and dangerous, assumption.

---

* During the credit crisis of 2008, the FDIC, the U.S. Treasury, and the Federal Reserve all took various actions that effectively increased the insured amount temporarily. At this writing, for example, the FDIC insurance limit is $250,000, all non–interest-bearing checking accounts are insured, and all money market fund balances are federally insured up to the amount invested as of September 19, 2008. The existence of these temporary increases does not invalidate the basic point.

HOW DO WE RECOGNIZE RISK?

Risk comes in many flavors. Some of these have already been touched on, and in the next chapter I will summarize the most important ones (see the section on portfolio theory). But in the big picture, when it comes to ferreting out investment risks there are only a few key points to remember:

1. Risk is everywhere.

2. Many risks are hidden.

3. Anything *you* do not understand is risky.

Risk is everywhere. Cultivate, as a foundational belief, the thought that "we are always taking risks when we do anything with our money." Make this an article of faith, a part of your mission statement. The more you become used to thinking this way, the better you will do at looking for and understanding the risks you are taking. In this context, it is more than okay to ask advisors or other service providers questions like "What happens if the company issuing this product fails?" or "Under what circumstances could we lose some or all of our principal in this investment?' If the advisor tells you, "That's not possible," you have another question to confront: How do you find a new advisor?

Many risks are hidden. What makes the topic of risk so difficult is that risks are hidden for all kinds of reasons, many (perhaps most) of which are innocent. At times, advisors themselves are unaware of one or more risks associated with the investments they recommend. The cure for this problem is a thorough dig into the relevant information. Board members rarely have the time or expertise to do their own research from scratch. However, they can, politely but persistently, require their advisors to provide detailed, convincing answers to questions about the risks inherent in a particular investment product, and to give adequate replies to follow-up questions. The usual result of this process is that everyone comes out smarter — not just the board, but the advisor, too.

PRACTICAL OBSERVATION 5
YOU CAN'T JUST READ THE SALES MATERIALS

To illustrate how an investment advisor can be caught unawares by the risks of an investment product, here is one quick story of a very close personal friend of mine who only read the sales materials.

Pacific Investment Management Company (PIMCO) is one of the largest fixed-income managers in the world. It invests hundreds of billions of dollars for institutions and, through mutual funds, for individuals. A while back, my friend wanted to add some unhedged international bonds to his personal portfolio, so he made an investment in the PIMCO Foreign Bond Fund (unhedged).

He knew a fair amount about PIMCO and its excellent reputation, and so did not tear the offering apart but rather did only a cursory review of its materials. Specifically, he read on the fund fact sheet (a two-page summary) that the fund held $2 billion-plus in "primarily high-quality, non-U.S. intermediate term bonds." Since that was just what he wanted, he bought into the fund.

A few months later, the subprime credit crisis hit. Many U.S. bonds and bond funds, particularly those with mortgage exposure, began losing value rapidly. My friend thought to himself, "Self. How clever you were to buy foreign bonds. They aren't caught up in the subprime crisis, and they won't drop in price like domestic corporate bonds." Then, to confirm his cleverness, he checked the prices on his holdings. To his shock, the price movement chart of his bond fund looked exactly like the price chart of any broad U.S. corporate bond fund at that time. It had lost 5 percent of its value in six weeks. Something was horribly wrong.

At this point, my friend started behaving like an investment professional (which he is) and belatedly did a very thorough review of the offering materials. There he found a schedule of fund holdings (which in fairness to PIMCO was published all along), showing $30 billion of assets offset by $28 billion of short positions. So it was a $2 billion foreign bond fund, *net,* but it also held billions of dollars of mortgaged-backed bonds, many of which were getting hammered in the credit crisis. This was why this so-called foreign bond fund was dropping in price right along with U.S. mortgage-backed bonds. The fund was more like a hedge fund than a simple portfolio of foreign bonds.

The moral of the story is that there is no substitute for thorough, traditional investment research. The PIMCO sales materials were not legally misleading or deceitful, as the information needed to make an informed decision was in fact there. It was just deeply buried in the details of a spreadsheet.

At the end of the day, my friend was the proverbial shoemaker whose children go barefoot. Although he would never do anything like this with a client account, for his own account he simply read the sales materials and consequently missed an important risk. Boy I sure won't do that again!

Anything you don't understand is risky. I think by now I've made the point that all investments come with risks. But those risks are amplified whenever you close your eyes, cut a corner or, most commonly, keep your doubts to yourself about an investment you don't understand. If you don't understand it, wait until you do. There is always another opportunity. This can, of course, be frustrating to advisors. They know there are directors in the world who are willfully stupid, who really don't want to understand a proposed investment and then use their confusion as a basis for rejecting the plan. But assuming you are a director who cares and is trying to do a good job: If you don't understand something you are being asked to approve, say so. I have had directors reject my investment suggestions a number of times. Let's assume, for the sake of conversation, that I was always right and they were always wrong. Nonetheless, I have never been upset with a board for saying no to something, because in virtually every case, the board's reluctance was an expression of discomfort with something they did not yet understand. To me, that simply meant I had more work to do educating the board and making my case. I don't begrudge the process and you shouldn't either. It's the way we learn and grow together.

CREATING HELPFUL POLICIES AND STRUCTURES

There is an essential difference between *doing* and *supervising*. In the context of this book, the distinction is between selecting specific investments for an organization and supervising (or holding accountable) those who actually do the selecting. My strong belief, based on 30 years in the financial services industry, is that those who supervise should not be the actual investors. To merge the two functions is to effectively eliminate accountability.

However, supervision does not imply passivity. There are a few steps board members must take, or cause to be taken, in order to discharge their legal and fiduciary responsibilities — as well as to build a structure that will best promote the organization's investment goals.

Those steps, as it happens, are all tied in the prudent investor laws (see Chapter 3) to the rules guiding proper delegation. Specifically, to correctly delegate investment authority, the board must

1. Adopt investment policies

2. Carefully screen the advisors it retains

3. Regularly review investment performance

The laws governing fiduciary investing now clearly provide that when a board takes these three steps, neither the organization nor the individual board members shall be liable for the actions of those to whom they delegate, nor for investment losses.

Adopt investment policies. The primary role of policies is to help everyone remember what the board has decided should be done. Written policies help everyone — board members, executive staff, and outside advisors — understand the organization's investment goals and the risks the organization is willing to take to achieve those goals.

Since perfection is not required, the first step is to adopt any policy and live with it for a while. You can always make changes based on your experience. Appendix I includes a simple set of policies that, as their author, I assure you are not perfect! But they are infinitely better than having no policy in place at all.

Hire advisors. Although the board should not be choosing among specific investments (everything from stocks and bonds to hedge funds and other, alternative investments), someone has to do it. Delegating this responsibility to someone else is not only permissible but preferable, assuming that the board is conscientious and careful in its choice. Chapter 5 discusses how to go about selecting an advisor.

Review performance. Hiring an investment advisor is not a one-time event. The board's legal responsibilities are not discharged unless the board (or its investment committee) regularly reviews the advisor's work and the organization's adherence to established policies in a disciplined manner. This is so central to sound investing that any qualified advisor should present a recommended review process as part of the package of services. (If the advisor does not recommend regular reviews, place one hand on your wallet and back slowly out of the room!)

Performance reporting and evaluation are discussed more thoroughly in the next chapter.

CONCLUSION

The good news is that the basics just reviewed represent a major portion of a board's duties in supervising investments. Adopt policies, hire an advisor, delegate supervision to an investment committee of the board (see Chapter 4), review, and repeat as necessary. None of this is conceptually difficult.

After the board has taken care of the basics, its job is to support the organization's staff, members, beneficiaries, and investment advisors by standing firm in its decisions and giving the basics time to work. This means, among other things, having the courage to stick to your guns during tough times, resisting impulsive policy changes, and refusing to allow the occasional downturn in results to cause hurried changes in allocations.

Having gone through the basics step by step helps a board resist the passions of the moment. No matter how emotional or fearful you might be, when you walk into a board meeting mindful of the careful reflection that went into your current policies, rational decision making becomes much easier. Through the policy-making process, we prepare ourselves and our organizations to strengthen the best in us and to temper our weaknesses. That, ultimately, is the reason to have an investment process that is reflected in investment policies.

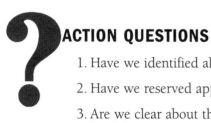

ACTION QUESTIONS

1. Have we identified all of our available funds to be invested?

2. Have we reserved appropriately for our ongoing cash flow requirements?

3. Are we clear about the specific goals and objectives for each of our separate funds?

4. Have we adequately balanced our tolerance for risk and our investment goals?

5. Are we satisfied that we know the risks we are already taking?

CHAPTER 2
INVESTMENT CONCEPTS FOR BOARD MEMBERS

There are only a few critical investment concepts every board member needs to understand:

- the meaning of *total return*

- the importance of *time* in managing money

- the role of *performance reporting* as a management tool

- the use of *portfolio theory* to control risks

- the circumstances in which portfolio theory is an inadequate risk management tool

If the last bullet point caught your attention, it should. I've thought long and hard about how to address the failure of so-called Modern Portfolio Theory in the early years of the 21st century. The essence of this widely used theory is that portfolios, which are simply collections of assets, can be structured in mathematically optimal ways to minimize the risk an investor is taking for a given level of anticipated return. And yet, a great many investors, individual and institutional, large and small, in recent years incurred investment losses that far exceeded their anticipated worst-case scenarios.

All of this chapter's treatment of key investment concepts remains valid in light of recent events. Investing for total return and carefully tracking results with appropriate performance reports continue to be sound practices. Even the use of portfolio theory to lessen risk is sound, as is the use of investment time frames to determine which risks to take. However, these practices will not prevent disaster in exceptional circumstances.[2] More important, even in normal times the standard methods have their limitations, which we must come to understand better. Portfolio theory is fine and, to some extent, helpful. By itself, however, it will not protect portfolios from substantial losses. If any one thing caused us to be surprised by the recent disastrous performance of the stock market, it was the belief that our

---

[2] Nassim Taleb, a former options trader now in academia, calls unexpected events that upset the normal order of things Black Swans. Taleb is one of the few writers in the financial world who accurately predicted the risk of a global meltdown involving the world's largest banks. His books — *Fooled by Randomness: The Hidden Role of Chance in Life and in the Markets* (2001) and *The Black Swan: The Impact of the Highly Improbable* (2007) — are entertaining and well worth reading.

techniques (and our advisors) were sophisticated enough to protect us. Once we know that's not the case, we can still use these techniques. We just need to expect less from them.

With that as preface, let's cover the first three bullet points above and then return to the topic of portfolio theory and its limitations.

TOTAL RETURN

Total return is the entire amount an investment earns, as opposed to just the current income produced (its *yield*). In other words, total return is the sum of dividends, interest, and capital gains, minus any expenses and capital losses. Frequently, the total return on an investment is quite different from the current yield.

By way of example, if you buy a 6 percent bond for $1,000 and hold it for one year, you will receive $60 in interest. But if you then sell the bond for $950, your true economic gain will be only $10 ($60 in interest payments reduced by a $50 capital loss). That is, you are paying out $1,000 and taking in, a year later, a net amount of $1,010. Consequently, the total return on your investment is only 1 percent, despite the bond's 6-percent designation. Measuring an investment on the basis of its total return is the only way to know with any accuracy how well or how poorly the investment is performing.

In the investment world, total return is usually measured annually on a calendar basis for individual investors, and on a trailing, quarterly basis for institutional accounts. To compute total return, the amount of capital gain or loss is determined by assuming that the investment was purchased on the first day of the year (or period in question) and sold on the last. To this capital gain or loss the total of all dividend or interest payments received for the period in question is added, and any expenses incurred (such as trading costs) are subtracted. Results are often reported both before and after investment management fees, if any.

One frequent objection to this way of measuring total return is that it treats unrealized gains and losses as if they were realized (i.e., as if the investment had been sold and an actual gain or loss were realized). Intuitively, an unrealized loss should not be as bad as a realized loss, since there is still the possibility that the unsold investment will regain its value. Why, for example, should it matter if a bond has decreased in value, if the investor intends to hold it to maturity?

There is a logic to this objection. However, when an investment has declined in value, if only temporarily, the organization has fewer assets on its books and less money available for its charitable purposes, no matter how certain the future appreciation may seem. In addition, there is an opportunity cost inherent in each investment. Continuing to hold an investment is essentially the same as deciding to buy that instrument instead of another. (This is particularly true in highly liquid markets with low commission costs.) If the organization wishes to switch to another investment, it can only do so with the reduced amount. No matter how confident an organization may be of its ability to sit on the investment and wait for its value to bounce back, the true current value is, literally, whatever the market will bear.

Today, virtually all investment advisors and all published indices report performance on a total return basis that includes both realized and unrealized gains and losses. This approach recognizes that there is almost always a possibility of the investor being forced to sell an investment. It also highlights losses much sooner than would be the case by other measurements.

Nonprofit accounting conventions now require the recognition of unrealized gains and losses in a nonprofit's financial records. In this regard, the accounting profession agrees with the investment community on the most accurate method of measuring total return. Any nonprofit board will want to understand this concept and measure its own investment performance by total return.

THE IMPORTANCE OF TIME IN MANAGING MONEY

Time often cures a multitude of sins. This is nowhere more evident than in the investment world. Those with patience are usually rewarded: There has been only one 15-year period since World War II during which the stock market lost money, and there are no 20-year periods. History thus suggests that even without the benefit of professional management or of risk-reducing asset allocations, a 100 percent investment in the stock market will make money, if given enough time.

This means that for endowments and other long-term funds with allocations to the equity markets, the longer the time frame the better. Unfortunately, our natural tendency is to think more short-term than is actually reasonable. In the institutional investment world, of which nonprofits are a part, consultants and investment committees commonly review a manager's performance quarterly. This is a good discipline. But equity portfolio managers as a group have very little control over quarterly returns. If they make good investments, the value of the portfolio will increase *over the long haul*. But it will not increase *every quarter,* and the dips and bumps are largely unpredictable.

For a board of directors and their investment committee, it is important to establish a relationship between the time frames applied to a particular portfolio and the board's risk tolerance. With endowments and other permanent funds, we may decide that three-year rolling numbers will be the primary performance measure. Since those funds have a perpetual investment horizon, intermediate-term volatility should not be a major concern. But to take that approach, we *absolutely must understand* how much our portfolio might decline in any shorter period of time and **then we need to be comfortable with that level of risk.** While intermediate-term volatility really should not matter, if we cannot sleep at night because of the declines in our portfolios, we will not be able to maintain our allocations in order to obtain the benefits of long-term investing.

PRACTICAL OBSERVATION 6
SOME SINS ARE WORSE THAN OTHERS

So long as they are sound sleepers, long-term investors can take greater risk and largely ignore intermediate-term volatility. However, this broad truth comes with several caveats.

For one thing, the short term does matter. On the road to those attractive long-term returns, we must be sure we can tolerate setbacks. That means avoiding losses so severe they threaten the health of the organization or force a radical change in allocations. If, for example, short-term losses affect our ability to secure a loan, we have a problem that can't be waved away by taking the long view.

Second, there have been times in the more distant past when markets were down for a long, long time. The graph on the next page shows the Dow Jones Industrial Average from 1929 to 1954. The Dow peaked in 1929 at 380. It next reached 380 in October of 1954, 25 years later. That's a pretty long "intermediate" term.

Finally, we also need to be mindful of something we could call the Law of Large Losses. When a portfolio declines in value, by definition you have a smaller capital base off which to earn returns. The math of large losses can be devastating. If a portfolio loses 25 percent of its value, that portfolio must earn $33^{1}/_{3}$ percent on the remaining capital just to get back to even. A 50 percent loss requires a 100 percent gain. That is the main reason it took the Dow of the 1930s 25 years to recover: With an 80 percent loss, getting back to even required a 400 percent return on the remaining capital!

So I increasingly find that while time does cure a multitude of sins, there are some sins I would just as soon avoid. Taking large losses is one of them. From that perspective, quarterly performance reporting, even on very long-term portfolios, is in fact appropriate. It confronts us with our losses sooner and forces us to consider whether or not we really can live with the risks we are taking.

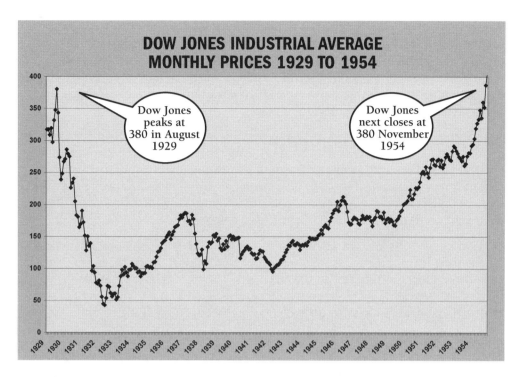

DOW JONES INDUSTRIAL AVERAGE MONTHLY PRICES 1929 TO 1954

Dow Jones peaks at 380 in August 1929

Dow Jones next closes at 380 November 1954

PERFORMANCE REPORTING AS AN INVESTMENT MANAGEMENT TOOL

Performance reports provide a reasonable and informed view of how well or poorly an organization's investments are doing. The best reports will also give us some idea of how much risk we have taken to achieve the results. Consequently, board members, and especially members of an investment committee, will typically want to spend significant time understanding and interpreting these reports. The committee's review of performance reports is an essential component of overall investment success.

It should be emphasized here that performance reporting is quite different from financial accounting. The latter is intended to convey an accurate reflection of organizational value at a given point in time. It is easy to confuse the two. In addition, it is important to distinguish between custodial statements and performance reports.

A **custodial statement** is a report, usually issued monthly, by the legal entity (e.g., bank, brokerage house, or trust company) that has custody of another's assets. It lists month-end values for all of the investments in an account. It also identifies unrealized gains and losses and itemizes all transactions that occurred during the period, including purchases and sales, additions or withdrawals of funds, and the payment of any expenses.

The purpose of a custodial report is to document the organization's assets with a statement that can be reconciled against internal records. This represents the absolute minimum information an organization should receive. To adequately discharge their supervisory duty, board members must also have reports that provide essential third-party information and historical data. This information is typically included in performance reports.

A **performance report** focuses on changes in the value of an investment account for a given period. In addition, such reports typically measure those changes against appropriate indices and, sometimes, against competing investment providers. More elaborate reports may also provide assessments of performance relative to risk. The most complex reports analyze performance through multiple statistical measures, in an attempt to identify the causes of success or failure.

Performance reports are typically provided quarterly. They usually show performance for the most recent quarter, as well as for the most recent calendar year, trailing year, or both. As longer histories of an organization's investments become available, the reports will typically cover longer trailing periods, such as three, five, and ten years. Most reports today use easy-to-understand graphics to help tell the story.

Portfolio performance can be measured against a wide variety of standard indices. There are narrow indices, such as the Dow Jones Industrial Average of 30 stocks, and broad indices, such as the Wilshire 5000, which is a weighted-average index of most publicly traded stocks in the United States for which price quotes are available. There are also "style" indices for specific equity categories, such as value, growth, and small-capitalization stocks, as well as numerous fixed-income and international indices.

It is important that you and your consultant choose an appropriate index, or blend of indices, against which to measure each of the organization's funds. Otherwise, you may be comparing apples to oranges. It would be misleading, for example, to compare a 50/50 mix of equities and bonds to the S&P 500, which is an all-stock index.

Because performance reporting can be somewhat complex, most board members will benefit from spending time with their consultant in order to obtain a full understanding of the reports. An advisor's guidance will be invaluable, for this is one area in which the time you spend developing greater knowledge will certainly pay off.

PRACTICAL OBSERVATION 7
2 + 2 = 4, 4.5, OR 5

In the real world, performance reporting is a bit of a bog. The first problem is that there are several different reasons to look at a report. We may want to know how well "we" are doing in the overall return on our portfolio or fund; or, on the other hand, we may want to know how well one or more of our managers are doing. The question of "our" performance tends to be absolute: Are we up or are we down? The question of a manager's performance, by contrast, tends to be relative: How is she doing compared to other managers, other funds, or an index in the same asset class? Thus, it's entirely possible to end up saying, "Our managers have done a great job" and, at the same time, "We lost 25 percent this year." In looking to a performance report for answers on how things are going with our money, we need to be clear about the questions we're asking.

The second source of muddle about performance reports is that different ways of calculating performance can produce very different results from the same set of transactions. Time-weighted returns, for example, measure investment performance in a way that is not affected by cash flows. This system is used for mutual fund and index reporting as well as for comparing managers to one another or to an index. Dollar-weighted returns, the other common performance measure, do take account of cash flows and therefore produce a number that will align more closely with the perceived changes in a portfolio's value whenever there are significant deposits or withdrawals. Be sure you understand the system your consultant is using and be sure that it is used consistently over time.

If you initially find performance reports confusing, don't worry. Over time you will come to understand them better. This is an area in which persistence pays off.

PORTFOLIO THEORY TO CONTROL RISK

At its most basic, risk is the possibility of a bad result. More technically, it is the measurable possibility of an investment losing, as opposed to gaining, value. There are numerous sources of risk. They include

- *individual-investment risk:* the risk associated with the decline in value of any one stock or bond. This is also called specific risk.

- *market risk:* the risk that all stocks and bonds in a particular market will decline in value

- *liquidity risk:* the possibility that market conditions preclude selling an asset

- *interest-rate risk:* the risk that changes in interest rates will cause capital losses in interest-rate–sensitive investments, such as bonds or preferred stock

- *inflation risk:* the risk that inflation will erode purchasing power and therefore the true return on an investment

- *currency risk:* the possibility that an investment denominated in a currency other than the U.S. dollar will decline in value when converted back into dollars, due to a relative decrease in the value of the other currency

Portfolio theory employs two major techniques to reduce risk:

Diversification is the distribution of investment funds among different instruments (typically stocks and/or bonds) for the purpose of reducing the *specific risk* associated with any one investment. A number of studies have shown that when a portfolio is diversified over 18 to 20 equity investments, more than 90 percent of specific risk is eliminated. In other words, having that many different securities in a portfolio will effectively eliminate the risk that any one stock can significantly diminish the portfolio's value.

However, effective diversification requires more than just having 20 different stocks in a portfolio. The equities must be in companies in different lines of business — because stocks of similar companies (which is to say, those in the same industry or sector) tend to respond in the same way to external economic events. A portfolio of 20 electric utility stocks or one of 20 airline stocks would not be adequately diversified to reduce risk. The stocks would tend to behave similarly in response to changes in interest rates, to increases in oil prices, or to other outside economic events. Sector diversification — being invested in different industry groups or sectors — is crucial to reducing risk.

The lack of sector diversification explains why those who invested heavily in high-flying dot-com or telecommunication stocks in the late 1990s were so badly hurt: They were concentrating their investments in narrowly focused stocks, mutual funds, or fund managers. When the limits of Internet profit potential, the overbuilding of fiber-optic networks, or the impact of deregulation in the telecommunication industry became apparent, the shares of all companies in that particular sector declined. In that situation, owning 20 or more different companies provided inadequate diversification.

Asset allocation is the distribution of investment funds among different classes of assets, such as stocks, bonds, foreign investments, real estate, commodities, and cash. **It can be thought of as diversification on a grand scale.** The theory underlying asset allocation is that asset classes will tend to react differently to the same outside economic events (referred to as *noncorrelation*). When investment managers refer to asset allocation, they mean the process of investing in different asset classes in order to reduce overall risk for a given level of anticipated return.

To take a simple example, if stocks go up when bonds go down, a portfolio consisting of stocks and bonds should have less risk than an all-stock portfolio. A similar relationship exists between U.S. stocks and cash investments, and between stocks and commodities. By focusing on how different asset classes behave, investors can minimize their risk for a given level of projected return.

Together, allocation among different asset classes and diversification of stocks and bonds among different industries and sectors can significantly reduce the risk in an organization's investment portfolio. They are not magic bullets (see the next Practical Observation), but they are valuable tools.

PRACTICAL OBSERVATION 8
DON'T BELIEVE EVERYTHING THE COMPUTER TELLS YOU

Every year people in the investment world spend countless hours producing asset allocation models using some form of mean variance optimization software. Those allocations suggest an optimal mix of assets for each set of risk and return numbers. You have undoubtedly seen the output, with recommendations that W percent be invested in large-cap growth stocks, X percent in value stocks, Y percent in foreign stocks, and Z percent in bonds.

The models recommend a mix of assets that may in fact improve performance of the portfolio over time. In that sense, the portfolio is "optimized." But optimized is not the same as "safe" or even "best," and an optimized portfolio may in fact not be much of a guide to either. The problems are legion.

For starters, the software works with the asset classes we give it. Stop, breathe, think. The software works only within the choices we allow. So if, for whatever reason, pure natural resource stocks are not "on our radar," the software cannot include those in its recommended allocations.

Second, all of our analysis is completely dependent on history. If, by way of example, we were building models in the year 2000, we might reasonably use 20 years of history, taking us back to 1980. Unfortunately, nothing in that 20 year period really compares with the tech stock collapse of 2001–2002 or the worldwide meltdown of 2008. The record is simply inadequate.

Finally, computer models are almost always constrained, by the people building them, to put some money in assets previously judged important. That is not a bad thing, but we tend to believe that anything produced by a computer and displayed in charts and graphs is a factual and accurate representation of the world. We tend to ignore, or not even consider, that it is just someone's well-dressed opinion. We are too easily dazzled by the math.

Our best course is to treat computerized portfolio analyses with caution and a healthy dose of skepticism. Various computerized models may well help us improve performance in normal times without necessarily protecting us in abnormal times. For that, we need the wisdom of directors and others who are willing to ask, "But what if it doesn't work?"

MODERN PORTFOLIO THEORY VS. REALITY

As noted in the preceding Practical Observation, there are important limitations to the tools the investment industry uses to construct recommended asset allocations, under the rubric of "Modern Portfolio Theory." More important, however, from a risk-management perspective there are important limitations on the theory itself. Two of these we will now consider.

Everything correlates in a crisis. The normal ways in which assets vary in price over time tend not to apply in a crisis. The chart below shows the S&P 500, the Nikkei 225, and the FTSE 100 (representing the U.S., Japanese, and U.K. stock markets, respectively) through the end of 2008. While the magnitude of change varies slightly from market to market, the direction of change is virtually identical. They all fell out of bed together. At least one explanation for this is that the people involved all over the world, the buyers and sellers of securities, now have access to the same information almost simultaneously. An individual investor in Dubai, a hedge fund manager in New York, and a retirement plan administrator in Sydney can all see the same markets at the same time if they wish. While I cannot prove it, I strongly suspect that widely shared information leads to correlated behavior.

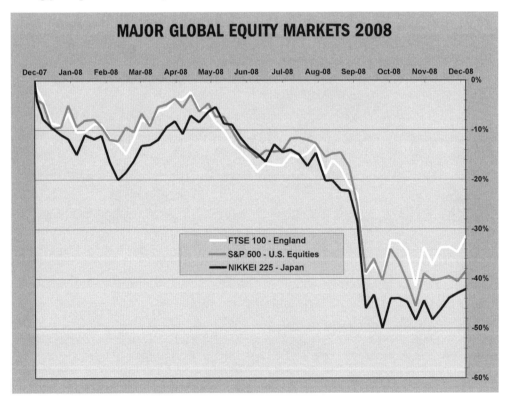

The next chart shows the S&P 500 again, but now in comparison to two exchange-traded commodities funds. DBA represents a basket of agricultural commodities (corn, wheat, soybeans, and sugar), while DBC represents a broader range of commodities (corn and wheat, but also crude oil, heating oil, aluminum, and gold). While the graphs are less strikingly parallel than those in the previous chart, commodities clearly dropped with the stock market, ending the year down 20 percent to 30 percent. The graphs illustrate how financial assets, meaning very broadly anything that can be bought and sold in a market, tend to correlate in a crisis.

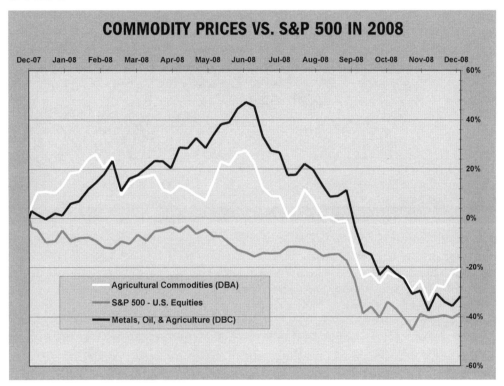

Finally, our third chart compares the S&P 500 to short-term U.S. Treasury bonds and gold. We can see that neither the short-term Treasury bonds nor gold were correlated to the stock market and that both in fact offered significant downside protection during the precipitous declines of 2008. From that we might be tempted to conclude that modern portfolio theory does work as advertised, you just have to pick the right asset classes. But that's not quite the whole story. The conundrum is that a portfolio allocated entirely to short-term Treasuries and gold would, in most markets and over many, many years, fail to provide adequate returns for future growth. At the same time, a portfolio allocated to almost anything else, would not have emerged undamaged from 2008. So while it is not literally true that *all* asset classes correlate in a crisis, it is close enough to true to make it difficult for us to blithely rely on modern portfolio theory as our safety net.

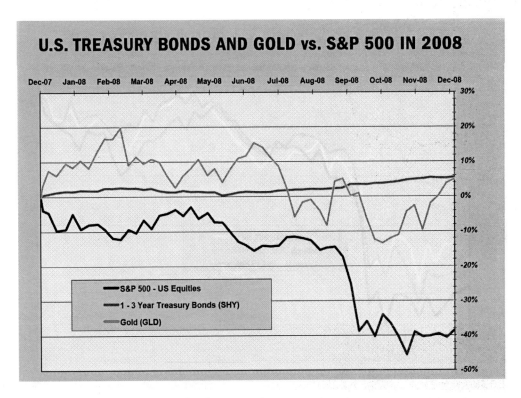

U.S. TREASURY BONDS AND GOLD vs. S&P 500 IN 2008

Legend:
- S&P 500 - US Equities
- 1 - 3 Year Treasury Bonds (SHY)
- Gold (GLD)

You cannot count on normal. The second point is that the unexpected does happen and, perhaps, more often than we think. (See Taleb, cited earlier.) Most asset allocation models, however, assume that things *in the future* will be somewhere in the land of "normal" *as defined by the observed past.* In that regard, virtually all commonly used investment management tools and strategies rely on past data. Whether we consciously think this or not, we are constantly assuming that the way stocks and bonds behaved in the past is a good guide to the way they will behave in the future. To the extent that the unexpected does happen, all we can really say to that is "maybe, and maybe not."

Portfolio theory is still helpful. It gives us a rational basis for combining assets into portfolios and it leads to other disciplines, such as performance reporting and rebalancing that also add value over time. And the principal tools of modern portfolio theory — diversification and asset allocation — do help reduce portfolio losses. But portfolio theory is not a panacea, and it is most certainly not a substitute for the ongoing exercise of good judgment.

So long as we are aware of and remember this limitation, it is OK to use the tools. But we have to also remember to ask ourselves and our advisors, "What happens if things aren't normal?" The answer to that question can then lead us to choose against the model. By that I mean, we might reduce our risk exposure more than our model suggests, or add asset classes that, based on our view of the future, we hope may perform better in critical times or even take actions outside of the portfolios themselves, such as reducing spending demands. We move, in other words, away from mechanical reliance on the theory toward an approach informed by our best judgments and ongoing review.

 ## ACTION QUESTIONS

1. Are we looking at our investments on a total return basis?

2. Do we have proper performance reporting systems in place?

3. Have we established a time horizon for each of our funds?

4. Are we appropriately diversified at both the individual investment and asset class level?

5. Does our primary advisor or consultant have at least some awareness that it is possible to be badly wrong?

CHAPTER 3
THE LEGAL ENVIRONMENT

For well over a century, the rule governing investments by fiduciaries was the so-called prudent man rule. In the last 30 years, however, the prudent *man* rule has largely been replaced by the prudent *investor* rule. This is no mere renaming for political correctness; it is a substantive change in the law as it applies in most states.

In this chapter, we will explore

- the prudent man rule as background

- today's prudent investor rule

- the costs of investment management

- fund pooling

- limitations of the prudent investor rule

- the constraint of broader fiduciary duty

BACKGROUND: THE PRUDENT MAN RULE

The prudent man rule traces its roots to a case heard by the Supreme Judicial Court of Massachusetts, *Harvard College v. Amory* (1830). The court ruled that, when investing, a trustee of funds

> is to observe how men of prudence, discretion, and intelligence manage their own affairs, not in regard to speculation, but in regard to the permanent disposition of their funds, considering the probable income, as well as the probable safety of the capital to be invested.

The prudent man rule sounded reasonable and accommodating, but over time it became more constrictive. As states began to codify the rule, their legislatures often went much further than the original decision in restricting investments by fiduciaries. Some laws actually specified lists of acceptable investments; these became known as *legal list* statutes. Other laws limited fiduciaries to investing in U.S. government securities and high-grade corporate bonds, prohibiting ownership of common stocks.

Judicial interpretation of the prudent man rule also tended to be cautious and conservative. Preservation of capital was accorded supreme importance. The board members' primary responsibility was never to lose money on the underlying investment. In addition, investments were expected to generate current income, which made non–income-producing assets suspect, if not outright inappropriate.

Most important, each investment was judged independently, not as part of a portfolio of investments. Board members could be liable for losses incurred on a single investment, even if the overall portfolio performance was excellent. In short, the laws and the courts' interpretations of them encouraged fiduciaries to adopt extremely conservative investment attitudes, usually entirely excluding any investment in common stocks.

The attitudes created during the heyday of the prudent man rule still linger in the nonprofit community. While it is today rare to find charitable organizations investing endowments or other longer-term funds exclusively in certificates of deposit or U.S. government bonds, there is still a widespread attitude that "charitable" means "more conservative than we might otherwise consider best." Since the new rules, described below, have now been in place in most states for more than 30 years, it is high time we come to terms with the investment freedom those new rules provide.

TIME FOR A CHANGE

The catalysts for a change in the law were rising inflation and the maturing of modern portfolio theory.

Throughout the 1950s and well into the 1960s, inflation remained modest — mostly less than 2 percent. Investors grew used to this climate and mostly didn't give the capital-eroding effects of inflation much thought. However, as inflation began climbing steadily, breaking 4 percent in 1968, holders of supposedly low-risk fixed-income portfolios began to worry about their declining purchasing power. If the trend were to continue, they would find the true value of their endowments radically reduced over time.[3] Both trustees and beneficiaries began questioning the wisdom of the restrictions under which they were operating.

At the same time, portfolio theory was moving out of academia and into practical application. Prompted by rising inflation, and using portfolio theory as an analytical tool, the Ford Foundation put out two notable studies — "The Law and the Lore of Endowment Funds" in 1969 and a companion study five years later — recommending clear rules that would allow universities (and by extension, all nonprofits) to "spend" principal and to invest for total return. These studies, and the publicity surrounding them, led directly to the widespread adoption of the prudent investor rule.

---

[3] The trend did continue. Inflation rose and fell, but mostly rose, in the 1970s and topped 14 percent in 1980.

THE PRUDENT INVESTOR RULE TODAY

The prudent investor rule today has two primary statutory expressions. The first is the Uniform Management of Institutional Funds Act (UMIFA), originally promulgated in 1972 and revised as the Uniform Prudent Management of Institutional Funds Act (UPMIFA) beginning in 2006. As this book goes to press, the UPMIFA has been adopted in 27 states and legislation is pending in four others. Its predecessor, the UMIFA, was ultimately adopted in 47 states.

The second expression of the prudent investor rule is the Uniform Prudent Investor Act (UPIA; 1992), which applies the principles to trusts. As of this writing, the UPIA has been adopted in 46 states. As a result, in most states, the funds of the organization itself — and any funds for which a charitable nonprofit serves as trustee — are governed by the same prudent-investor standards.

Even in the few states that have not adopted these uniform laws, the same principles usually apply. In 1990, the American Law Institute issued a Restatement of the investment-standards portion of the Law of Trusts, which incorporated prudent-investor thinking. (*The Restatement of the Law of Trusts* is a "common law" guide to attorneys and judges in states without those statutes.) Consequently, while every organization needs to check with its attorney on exactly what laws apply in its state, some version of the prudent investor rules is almost certainly in effect.

EXAMINATION OF THE LEGAL RULES

In updating the UMIFA, the drafters of the new Act intentionally followed the UPIA so that both laws now have very similar language and more clearly agree on general fiduciary investment standards. ***The discussion below focuses primarily on UPMIFA, as the statute that applies most directly to the management of nonprofit funds.*** Appendix IV includes a copy of the new law.

It is interesting to note that the National Conference of Commissioners on Uniform State Laws, headquartered in Chicago, Illinois, is one of those quasi-government organizations, unknown to most people, that quietly does excellent work of enormous benefit to our country. To quote from their Web site,

> The National Conference of Commissioners on Uniform State Laws (NCCUSL), now in its 116th year, provides states with non-partisan, well-conceived and well-drafted legislation that brings clarity and stability to critical areas of state statutory law.

The Web site, www.nccusl.org, is an excellent source of current information on all of the laws discussed in this book and provides an easy way to check which laws have been enacted in your state.

STANDARD OF CARE

Section 3 of the UPMIFA establishes the standard of care for managing funds, called by the Act the "Standard or Conduct in Managing and Investing Institutional Funds." (All quoted language is from the UPMIFA.)

The Act begins with the language, "subject to the intent of the donor in a gift instrument," as a means of clarifying that specific directions from donors in specific instruments can still overrule the general guidance provided by the Act. It goes on to establish that the basic standard is, as it has always been, that

> each person responsible for managing and investing an institutional fund shall manage and invest the fund in good faith and with the care an ordinarily prudent person in a like position would exercise under similar circumstances.

You will recognize the similarity of this language to that of *Harvard College v. Amory,* penned 176 years earlier. Somehow I find that comforting.

Taking a page now from the slightly older UPIA, the new Act specifies some of the factors one may consider in determining prudence. Specifically, the Act provides:

1. In managing and investing an institutional fund, the following factors, if relevant, must be considered:

   (A) general economic conditions;

   (B) the possible effect of inflation or deflation;

   (C) the expected tax consequences, if any, of investment decisions or strategies;

   (D) the role that each investment or course of action plays within the overall investment portfolio of the fund;

   (E) the expected total return from income and the appreciation of investments;

   (F) other resources of the institution;

   (G) the needs of the institution and the fund to make distributions and to preserve capital; and

   (H) an asset's special relationship or special value, if any, to the charitable purposes of the institution.

Again, the reader will recognize that the Act incorporates many of the important investment concepts we have already discussed including inflation, portfolio theory, total return and liquidity. This is part and parcel of what makes it possible for charities to invest reasonably in today's world. That which is in fact best is reflected in the governing laws.

Three investment concepts are so important that they get special mention in the Act. The first is the notion of judging prudence based on the aggregate actions as opposed to the old Prudent Man standard that judged investments individually. In that regard, the Act provides

2. Management and investment decisions about an individual asset must be made not in isolation but rather in the context of the institutional fund's portfolio of investments as a whole and as a part of an overall investment strategy having risk and return objectives reasonably suited to the fund and to the institution.

Second, the Act eliminates any doubt that there is such a thing as an investment that is inappropriate per se. Here the Act provides

3. Except as otherwise provided by law other than this [act], an institution may invest in any kind of property or type of investment consistent with this section.

Finally, in an acknowledgement of both common sense and hundreds of years of common law, the Act mandates diversification as follows:

4. An institution shall diversify the investments of an institutional fund unless the institution reasonably determines that, because of special circumstances, the purposes of the fund are better served without diversification.

DELEGATION OF AUTHORITY

The new Act continues to articulate and clarify that it is appropriate for organizations to delegate investment services to third parties. Specifically:

(a) An institution may delegate to an external agent the management and investment of an institutional fund to the extent that an institution could prudently delegate under the circumstances.

To do this properly, however:

An institution shall act in good faith, with the care that an ordinarily prudent person in a like position would exercise under similar circumstances, in

(1) selecting an agent;

(2) establishing the scope and terms of the delegation, consistent with the purposes of the institution and the institutional fund; and

(3) periodically reviewing the agent's actions in order to monitor the agent's performance and compliance with the scope and terms of the delegation.

What do those three rules actually require? You need to be diligent in selecting an agent, you need to be clear in giving that agent instructions, which is shorthand for having adopted investment policies that guide each agent's actions, and, you need to regularly review performance. Once again, the basics.

The Act then incorporates the good news as follows:

(c) An institution that complies with subsection (a) is not liable for the decisions or actions of an agent to which the function was delegated.

In establishing that the organization is not liable for the properly chosen, instructed and supervised agents, the Act also effectively relieves individual directors of liability.

CASE STUDY
APPROPRIATE DELEGATION

The new chief executive of a midsized nonprofit has had a considerable amount of investment experience, both personally and in previous jobs at other nonprofits. He has a more extensive and sophisticated knowledge of investment than any current board member. He has offered to relieve the board members of the burden of supervision of their investment advisor, to perform the work of the board's investment committee, and to report to the board at its semiannual meetings.

What concerns are raised by this proposal to delegate its authority to the chief executive?

First, no matter how capable the chief executive, the board is ultimately responsible for the investment decisions — by law and custom. Therefore a meaningful level of review of the chief executive's activities and decisions on investing is required. Is that satisfied by a semiannual report by the chief executive to the board? The board members decide, quite rightly, that it is not.

Are more heads better than one?

The board members also felt that regular participation by some of them on an investment committee — even if they were less knowledgeable than the chief executive — would bring more balance, common sense, and thoughtfulness to decision making than one very busy chief executive acting alone.

Finally, the board decided that is was wrong to ask their chief executive to properly judge the risk tolerance of the board and to make the other basic decisions on which investments would be made, if it was not sufficiently engaged in the process. Rather than abdicating all these responsibilities, the board voted to retain its investment committee — but added the chief executive to its membership.

COSTS OF INVESTMENT MANAGEMENT

In updating the UMIFA, the UPMIFA (drawing on the UPIA) now provides that:

(c) In managing and investing an institutional fund, an institution:

(1) may incur only costs that are appropriate and reasonable in relation to the assets, the purposes of the institution, and the skills available to the institution; and

(2) shall make a reasonable effort to verify facts relevant to the management and investment of the fund.

I suspect that these two items are presented together in the Act to basically make the point that you can delegate and you can hire help, but you cannot do so blindly. You need to know what you are doing (i.e., verify the facts) and you need to believe that what you are spending is reasonable. As much as these two rules sound like common sense, the answers in practice are not always obvious. (See Practical Observation 9.)

PRACTICAL OBSERVATION 9
"HOW MUCH DOES IT COST?" IS THE WRONG QUESTION

Investment costs are a hot topic in the nonprofit world, as elsewhere. At one end of the cost spectrum is the index fund, an unmanaged (hence, low-overhead) basket of securities chosen to mimic an index, such as the S&P 500. The last time I checked, the expense ratio on Vanguard's S&P 500 Index fund was only 7 basis points, meaning 7/100ths of 1 percent. That's really cheap.

At the other end of the spectrum are hedge funds, typically available only to institutional and high-net-worth investors. (See the Alternative Investments discussion in Chapter 6.) Here, a "typical" fee might be anywhere from "1 and 10" to "2 and 20." Those fees mean 1 percent or 2 percent of assets under management as an ongoing *fee* plus 10 percent or 20 percent of profits generated. If, as is not uncommon, the institution invests through a "fund of funds," which is a fund that holds interests in multiple hedge funds, that fund of funds may again charge "1 and 10," or some such. Add it all up and the fees on the fund of hedge funds might be as much as 3 percent of net asset value and 30 percent of profits. That's really expensive.

Why would you ever use a fund of hedge funds when you can buy index funds for a fraction of the cost? In one form or another, that question comes up all the time. Many, many directors and many potential donors want to know how much you are spending when managing your funds. The problem is that any cost and fee discussion, taken out of context, is almost always misleading.

Let's briefly examine a single, clarifying illustration. In 2008, the least expensive S&P 500 index fund would have declined by roughly 38 percent. At the same time, the median decline of broadly diversified funds of hedge funds was approximately 22 percent as measured by the Barclay Fund of Funds index. Even if you took another 3 percent in fees from the hedge fund numbers the difference in performance, net, was at least 13 percent which translates into *portfolio savings* of $130,000 per million dollars under management. In hindsight, looking at the fees in context makes the admittedly very high hedge fund fees seem a bit more reasonable.

The point is that costs and fees do matter but they cannot be analyzed alone or out of context. The least expensive option, as we know from many other areas of life, is not necessarily best. Who tries to have their coronary bypass performed by the lowest-cost heart surgeon?

In the context of our consulting work, we handle the cost and fee issue by both tracking it carefully and by reporting performance, net of all costs and fees. That at least assures some context for the question and helps focus on the real question which is, "Are we getting our money's worth from the managers and funds we are using?"

FUND POOLING

Finally, the new Act also makes it clear that institutions may pool funds for investment management purposes. Specifically, the Act provides

> (d) An institution may pool two or more institutional funds for purposes of management and investment.

This is really very good news in that there are tremendous advantages to pooling funds. The advantages are largely administrative. Every separately managed account requires a custodial relationship, an investment management contract, and performance reports. Take $10,000,000 and manage it as a single pool and you potentially have only one set of costs. Even if you use multiple managers for different asset classes, you can still hold all the accounts at the same institution and aggregate them for both fee and performance reporting purposes.

Take that same "pool" and break it down into managed accounts for each interested party, and you can end up with twenty $500,000 relationships ... or worse. In that event you have 20 or more of everything and almost certainly higher investment management costs besides. All in all, pooling of investments is invariably a major benefit to an institution in both reducing costs and improving performance.

LIMITS OF THE UNIFORM ACTS

As you may properly infer from the foregoing discussion of the prudent-investor laws, almost nothing is prohibited outright, which means that virtually any investment is available to nonprofits. Therefore, common stocks of all types (large, small, domestic, and foreign), private placements, hedge funds, and derivatives are all fair game. Investment prudence is to be judged in the aggregate, not one investment at a time. In this world, the new challenge is managing the multiplicity of choices.

There are, however, a few important exceptions to this general rule as a result of either (a) the incomplete adoption of prudent-investor concepts, or (b) the existence of special rules (usually tax-related) that apply to certain organizations or in certain circumstances.

First, the so-called *uniform acts* are legislative proposals recommended to the states for enactment by a drafting commission. While most states have adopted these proposals, not all have and not all have adopted the acts in their entirety or without important changes. (The legislature of my home state of California, for example, almost always makes changes in the proposed language when adopting a uniform act.) Therefore, it is vital to learn from your legal counsel exactly what laws and concepts apply in your state.

Second, the old prudent-man concept has been embedded in jurisprudence for so many years that it still lies tucked away in unsuspected corners of statutes in many states. In a number of states, for example, the investment of gift-annuity reserves is still governed by anachronistic prudent-man concepts. Again, advice of counsel is the best way to keep from being blind-sided by a prudent-man provision.

Some tax laws, federal and state, place restrictions — explicit or implicit — on nonprofits. In 1969, Congress adopted what were then new tax rules for private foundations, charitable-remainder trusts, and charitable-lead trusts. Those rules contain a handful of investment restrictions. Private foundations, for example, are not allowed to make *jeopardy investments*. The term applies to investments that are so inherently risky that they might jeopardize the viability of the organization. Unfortunately, the term jeopardy investment is not clearly defined in either the code or the regulations.

The language of the IRS review manual on the subject is not at all encouraging. While first acknowledging that, "no category of investments is to be treated as a per se violation of IRC 4944 [so] there are no specific investments that are treated as jeopardizing investments," it goes on to say, "There are, however, examples of types or methods of investments which require close scrutiny to determine whether foundation managers have met the requisite standard of ordinary business care and prudence." Among the examples of methods that require close scrutiny are trading in commodity futures, using hedge funds or derivatives, or investing in the international equities of developing countries.

Suffice it to say that since no one wants "close scrutiny" from the IRS, there is an understandable hesitancy on the part of private foundations to utilize any one of a number of what would otherwise be considered mainline, modern investment instruments and strategies.

THE CONSTRAINT OF BROADER FIDUCIARY DUTY

While UPMIFA and UPIA provide specific guidance for directors and trustees, general, common-law duties also arise out of trust relationships, either express or implied.

For the sake of our conversation, "A fiduciary is a person or an entity who holds a trust relationship to another. Anyone who controls assets or exercises power or authority for the benefit of someone else is said to be a 'fiduciary,' and such a person's responsibilities are referred to as 'fiduciary duties.' It is a very broad concept with deep roots in Anglo-American law."[4] If a nonprofit organization serves as trustee for a charitable trust, that organization as a trustee owes a fiduciary duty to the beneficiaries, who are those people or entities for whose benefit the trust exists.

Fiduciary duty is an even broader concept in the nonprofit world because, in most states, such duty is an express part of the laws governing nonprofit organizations. Specifically, nonprofits are deemed to be holding **all** of their assets, including investment funds, in trust for the benefit of the constituencies and the charitable purposes for which the organization exists. The state attorney general is typically given broad authority to enforce the trust concept and to prevent the theft, misuse, or mismanagement of a nonprofit organization's funds.

The concept of fiduciary duty infuses all aspects of nonprofit investment management, as a complement to specific investment laws like UPMIFA. In practice, it means that even if a particular investment is appropriate under prudent-investor concepts, that investment still might not be appropriate if, for whatever reason, the action was not in the best interest of those for whom the funds are being managed. Fiduciary duty is the ultimate constraint on what is otherwise a very liberal, modern investment environment created by the prudent investor rule.

ACTION QUESTIONS

1. Do we understand the changes between the prudent man rule and prudent investor rule and how the differences affect our investment flexibility?

2. Have we protected ourselves from liability by delegating the investment authority to a qualified outside expert?

3. Do we hold any assets such as gift annuity reserves where the normal prudent investor rules might not apply?

4. Does our investment committee understand its fiduciary role?

5. Are we prepared to discuss our investment costs and fees in the context of overall portfolio performance?

[4] Fry, Robert P., Jr. *Nonprofit Investment Policies: Practical Steps for Growing Charitable Funds.* Hoboken, NJ: John Wiley & Sons, 1998.

CHAPTER 4
UNIQUE ISSUES FACING NONPROFITS

Nonprofit organizations can benefit from investment theory, methods, and practices developed by the for-profit world. However, there are significant differences between charitable organizations and for-profit companies. Some of these differences work to a nonprofit's advantage, such as the willingness of very competent people to serve as directors on an investment committee. But some of the differences, such as mandated spending policies, are effectively restraints on organizational freedom. In all cases, it will be helpful for the board to understand that which is unique and to see that those differences are reflected in the organization's investment policies and procedures.

Some of the more important differences include the following:

- the critical role of an investment committee

- the existence of many different sources of funds under management

- the interaction between investment policy and donors

- socially responsible investing

- scam-proofing

- the importance of spending policies

- the need to be mindful of conflicts of interest

THE ROLE OF AN INVESTMENT COMMITTEE

In any corporation, nonprofit or otherwise, ultimate responsibility for the health and well-being of the entity rests with the board of directors. But as a practical matter, most boards delegate the actual authority over more complex operations to committees or to its executive staff. This is often the case with investments. An investment committee is, typically, a smaller committee of board members that may also include additional non–directors as committee members. While there are many variations of how investment committees are established, it is not uncommon for the nonprofit's chief financial officer to chair the committee and to act as a conduit between the committee and those delegated to do the actual work.

Under most state corporation laws, a board can delegate its authority to properly constituted committees. Therefore, an investment committee can largely serve in the board's place in supervising the investment process. I have already shared my strong opinion that directors should supervise and not actually manage funds themselves. Direct management by board members effectively eliminates independent supervision. The reason to stress the role of an investment committee is that it facilitates the supervisory process by allowing the work to be done by those directors who have the time, interest, and knowledge that such supervision requires.

The committee will typically receive and review the performance reports submitted by its staff and outside advisors, meet quarterly (or at least annually) with the primary consultant and participate in other meetings or reviews as needed. How active the committee might be will depend on the size of the organization, the complexity of the investments, and the presence or absence of internal staff available to assist. In doing this work, the committee is satisfying the prudent-investor requirement of ongoing supervision of outside advisors and is thereby protecting both the organization and the other directors from liability.

PRACTICAL OBSERVATION 10
IT'S GREAT TO HAVE SOMEONE TO TALK TO

As an advisor, I love it when the client organization has an investment committee of the board. The existence of such a committee almost always improves the quality and depth of the conversations and, by extension, the quality and depth of the supervision and review. This is a very important and practical point: People serve on nonprofit boards for all kinds of good and valid reasons. Some directors are experts in whatever the core work or ministry of the nonprofit happens to be. Others bring particular expertise in areas of law, government, or public relations. And some, the most important of all, are great fundraisers! But it is entirely possible that only a handful of those folks actually know much about investing. If the entire board tries to supervise the investment team, the gap in knowledge between directors can be an ordeal for everyone. One director asks why we are paying our bond manager 50 basis points, suggesting that in his experience that is too high, while another director asks, "What's a basis point?" (A basis point is 1/100th of 1 percent.) The conversation pretty much grinds to a halt at that moment.

Having an investment committee lets the advisor and committee members get to know each other over time. With each meeting, a little greater depth of understanding and trust can develop. Objections are remembered and addressed, successes celebrated, failures considered ... without the glare of folks who may not have been involved in the decisions or understand the choices that were made. It's a great structure, which I heartily recommend.

SOURCE AND CHARACTER OF FUNDS

As noted in Chapter 1, there are many different types of charitable assets including operating reserves, retirement funds, capital campaign funds, endowments and interests in planned gifts. Each different type of fund can have a slightly different character from an investment perspective, including time horizons, liquidity needs, risk profile, interested parties, and, surprisingly, tax considerations. Let's briefly comment on each of these characteristics or attributes.

Before proceeding, however, we should first note that this discussion is not about fund accounting. That is an accounting concept by which nonprofits track their funds and under which they are required to categorize their funds as *unrestricted, temporarily restricted,* or *permanently restricted.* These categories are intended to describe an organization's *access* to the funds for audited financial statement purposes but not to tell the organization *how* the various funds in question should be invested.

TIME HORIZONS

The first important question is the length of time for which the funds will be invested. Broadly speaking, *operating reserves* include any funds being held for general spending within the next 12 months with everything else representing *longer-term funds.* Usually these distinctions are fairly clear with the checking account being part of the operating reserve and a permanent endowment representing longer-term funds. But that is not always the case. We have already noted that capital campaign funds are an example of something that can be held longer than we originally intended. On the other hand, money in a donor advised fund might be held for a shorter period than we had planned due to a donor's decision to distribute the funds sooner rather than later. All we can really say on this subject is that part of the investment process is a conscious review and monitoring of the time horizons associated with each fund.

LIQUIDITY NEEDS

While liquidity is often closely tied to investment time horizons, they are not always the same. Even endowment funds with perpetual time horizons still, typically, make quarterly distributions for which cash must be available. In the planned gift arena in particular, each different type of trust can have a different liquidity requirement. And sometimes the requirement can change as a result of some specific event. There are, for example, charitable remainder trusts that on the occurrence of a specified event switch from distributing their net income (which may be zero) to distributing a percentage of net asset value. In that event, the liquidity requirement could increase significantly even though the time horizon was unchanged. Here, again, monitoring is the order of the day.

INTERESTED PARTIES, RISK PROFILES AND TAX CHARACTERISTICS

Largely these varying interests again arise in the planned gift arena. Both Charitable Remainder Trusts and Charitable Lead Trusts are so-called split interest trusts in which there is a charitable interest and an interest held by one or more individuals. If your organization manages such trusts as a trustee or otherwise, it is extremely important that the investment team is aware of the interests of the different parties.

INTERACTION BETWEEN INVESTMENT POLICY AND DONORS

Nonprofits are different from for-profit companies in their dependence on and relationships with donors and other constituents. Frequently, an organization's donors are partners in the work and mission of the organization, giving of themselves as volunteers and supporting the organization in many other ways (besides just writing checks). Understanding how investment policies may impact donors, and vice versa, is important for a nonprofit board.

GIVING DONORS CONFIDENCE

Whether a donor contributes five dollars or $5 million, she is entrusting her gift to a nonprofit in the belief that the organization will use the money wisely to accomplish the nonprofit's mission or ministry. To the extent that the organization has a surplus or maintains an endowment, having an investment policy in place is one of the most important things the board can do to give donors confidence in the soundness of the organization's management. It is a way to assure donors that their trust will not be betrayed through sloppiness or neglect.

GIFT-ACCEPTANCE POLICIES

Most assets of a nonprofit start out as gifts. If the gift is cash, no particular issues are raised beyond proper accounting and record keeping. But what about gifts of publicly traded stock?

Tax law provides strong incentives to donors to give gifts of appreciated stock directly, instead of selling the stock and donating the cash. For gifts of appreciated publicly-traded stock, the donor receives an income-tax charitable deduction for the full fair market value of the gifted shares without having to pay any tax on the embedded capital gains. From a tax perspective, that is a very wise and efficient way to make charitable gifts.

Consequently, gifts of appreciated stock are becoming more common. How, then, should a nonprofit handle these gifts? Normally, stock gifts should simply be sold upon receipt. If the organization has an advisor who is maintaining a stock portfolio, the gifts can be directed to the investment advisor for evaluation. The only question the advisor really needs to answer is: Would the nonprofit normally hold such a position in its portfolio? If the answer is "no," the stock should be sold, as the only cost of doing so will be the relatively minor sales charges, if any.

To do otherwise (e.g., to keep shares simply because they were donated to the nonprofit) is essentially to abandon investment discipline. A large gift of stock to a small organization, for example, can skew the portfolio toward a particular sector or industry. It can also result in inadequate diversification that puts the nonprofit's investments at greater risk. Whatever the impact may be, it is almost certain that it will not be an investment anticipated by the organization's investment strategy.

Wealthy donors sometimes have a high opinion of their own investment knowledge. By having both investment and gift acceptance policies in place ahead of time, it is much easier to inform major donors of the intended disposition of their gift of shares — without having that action seem personal or critical.

PRACTICAL OBSERVATION 11
SOMETIMES YOU CAN'T SELL IT QUICKLY ENOUGH

Some stock gifts can be very difficult to sell, which can cause donor relationship problems. For income tax purposes, the IRS has a very clear formula for valuing gifts of publicly-traded stock. Under that formula, the value for tax purposes is the average of the high and low prices of the shares in the market for the day that is determined to be the valuation date. Normally, the valuation date is the day the shares are received by the organization or its agents, but it can also be the day the shares are mailed. The IRS publications go on to explain how to establish value if there were no trades that particular day.

The most important point for our purposes is that the IRS has an approach for determining value, which is very reasonable but which may not be the amount that your organization receives in cash when it sells the shares. If the stock gift represents an extremely large position relative to the number of shares that trade, it may not be possible to sell the shares on the day they are received. If the stock has a very low price or is very thinly traded, it can take days or weeks or even longer to sell a large block.

Normally, this is not a problem as it merely affects the amount of money that the nonprofit ultimately receives for the gift. But there can be situations in which the donor cares about the amount that is realized from the sale. If, for example, the gift is intended to establish a named endowment, then the donor will want to know how much money is in the endowment after the sale of the shares. If the endowment ends up with only $25,000 shortly after the donor receives a tax statement showing that she made a gift of $50,0000, she will understandably want to know where the rest of the money went. The truth is, it didn't go anywhere. The tax statement reports a value based on tax rules and the market delivers a value based on the realities of the sale. These can be very different.

Because the problem is one of markets, there is no perfect cure. Ideally, someone should be in a position to review such gifts the moment they are received or, better still, before they are received, in order to advise the donor of the true value of the gift. Most commonly, this is a matter of expectation management as much as anything.

GIFTS OF ILLIQUID ASSETS

Sometimes a donor will want to contribute an asset other than stocks or bonds. These gifts might include *hard* assets, such as real estate, art, or jewelry; or *intangible* assets, such as mineral interests, closely held stock, or intellectual property. Such gifts are more difficult to handle than publicly traded stocks and bonds because they are often highly illiquid.

Before accepting such a gift, a nonprofit should secure a professional evaluation of the gift that would include valuation, marketability, storage and insurance costs, and other potential liabilities, such as environmental matters. With gifts of real estate, for example, it is possible for environmental liabilities to exceed the value of the property.

Most gifts of this kind, if accepted, should be sold immediately and not held as an investment, unless there is a specific mission or ministry reason for doing so (e.g., the gift of a building appropriate for the organization's use).

Some organizations have great expertise in this area. The National Christian Foundation (NCF) in Atlanta, for whom I serve as chief investment advisor, has tremendous expertise in facilitating gifts of illiquid assets. Donors can use NCF to receive illiquid assets, effect the sale of those assets, and place the proceeds into a fund from which the donor may recommend future distributions to one or more end-user charities. There are a handful of other community foundations of one sort or another who have similar expertise. Taking advantage of such expertise can be an excellent way for smaller charities to improve their ability to receive gifts of illiquid assets.

SOCIALLY-RESPONSIBLE INVESTING

In recent years, a growing number of nonprofits have included "socially responsible" guidelines in their investment policies. This is an effort to align the investment of an organization's funds with its ministry or mission. It is an effort that is difficult to execute but nonetheless has wide-ranging support across the religious and political spectrum. The effort to align investment policy and social or ministry policy fall broadly into three categories: Portfolio Screening, Shareholder Activism, and Program-Related Investing.

PORTFOLIO SCREENING

The most popular approach to social or moral investing is portfolio screening. Many nonprofits attempt to "screen" their investments to eliminate those that are inconsistent with their missions. For many organizations, it is important to make this effort. The most common companies avoided are those involved in tobacco, alcohol, gambling, pornography, and weapons production.

Within reasonable limits, screening based on social and moral criteria is feasible. Advisors can accommodate social screens in individually managed accounts by either maintaining restricted lists internally or by outsourcing that work to social research firms. So long as the list is not excessive, your advisors should be able to honor such requests.

Organizations that screen investments are making a statement that reflects the organization's positions and values. As such, it can be very important. But we should also recognize the limitations of screening and realize that purity is not possible.

One limitation is the sheer complexity of capital markets in our now global economy. Even with computerized databases and vast quantities of research, it is still a daunting task to ferret out all the activities of major corporations. Additionally, screening is virtually impossible through index funds and most mainstream mutual funds because of their broad holdings (although there are some socially responsible mutual funds). Finally, I have yet to see a nonprofit investment policy that prohibits holding U.S. government securities, which are usually the essential core of a fixed-income portfolio. Any organization that owns federal bonds but is concerned about alcohol, tobacco, gambling, nuclear energy, or armaments, is "investing" in each of those activities, as the federal government is either an active participant or a silent partner in all. So organizations screen investments more for advocacy than for efficacy.

SHAREHOLDER ADVOCACY

Another form of social advocacy is, literally, shareholder advocacy. As shareowners of publicly traded companies, nonprofits have a voice and vote through the annual meeting proxy voting system. In this context, organizations can use their investments to lobby for positive changes in the global economy, environment, and culture. In recent years, nonprofits have participated in hundreds of shareholder resolutions addressing everything from executive compensation to disclosure of environmental impacts.

PROGRAM-RELATED INVESTMENTS

Perhaps the most interesting (and newest) approach to socially-responsible investing is direct investment in for-profit companies working to correct a social ill or conducting business in a manner that is consistent with the nonprofit's mission and purposes. Investments of this type have been made over the years, largely by grantmaking foundations, under the name of program-related investments (PRIs).

In recent years, some donors have turned their entrepreneurial energies to helping nonprofits invest in their missions as opposed to simply donating money. Some of these efforts have led to the creation of entirely new for-profit organizations that are owned by or in some other way support the nonprofit enterprise. The result of these investments can be excellent for both donor and organization. For the donor, creating a whole new company represents a far higher level of personal participation, commitment, and, potentially, satisfaction. For the organization, such enterprises can represent a new source of ongoing funding.

Program-related investing is most well-developed in the areas of housing and microfinance. In the housing space, a number of larger organizations have created entire programs to provide low-cost loans for inner-city residents or for developers building low-income housing. In the microfinance space, some companies, have garnered enormous publicity and attention (including a Nobel Prize to Grameen Bank and its founder, Muhammad Yunus) for the poverty-reducing impact of microfinance loans. (For a broader discussion, see the Suggested Resources.) It is an intriguing area. There can, however, be some real challenges in this area, as discussed in our next Practical Observation.

PRACTICAL OBSERVATION 12
ARE WE MAKING AN INVESTMENT OR A GRANT?

I love the whole area of program-related investments and, indeed, the whole notion of trying to invest in companies that are producing both profits and social benefits. There are ministry-minded companies working on water projects, health care, microfinance, and other areas. Currently, by way of example, my firm is attempting to structure an investment in a group that is building a for-profit hospital in Western China. All these groups are attempting to achieve social goals but to do so profitably. And there's the rub.

When it comes to evaluating program-related investments of whatever sort, we need to be mindful of our primary fiduciary responsibilities. If someone has entrusted us with investment responsibility for his retirement funds, we cannot properly go and invest those funds in an African water purification company, no matter how noble their goals, unless we believe we are acting in the absolute best interest of those we are charged to serve. It is very easy to allow our good hearts and our good emotions to lead us down a very bad investment path. I've been there and done that personally a number of times!

So what is the answer? I believe the best approach is to segregate funds into those for which we are maximizing risk-adjusted returns — period — and those with which we can take greater risk for the sake of a mission or ministry objective. Once we have deliberately set aside some portion of our assets for investment in a mission-motivated venture, we have already avoided the first problem, which is inadvertence; we're doing this on purpose. That should facilitate the further discussion of whether or not we would be in breach of any other duty if we were to lose these funds in their entirety. If that would not be the case, then we have probably identified and segregated the right amount of funds. By taking this approach, a board may pursue its true heart's desire in terms of social service while avoiding the temptation to take inappropriate investment risks with what is, truly, some else's money.

SCAM-PROOFING

Another ongoing problem that is common, if not unique, to the nonprofit space is the proliferation of fundraising and investment scams. The fundraising world is a tough one, in which scam artists and smooth talkers mingle among the vast majority of legitimate and dedicated people. The pressure on nonprofit executives and staff may make them vulnerable to ventures that are questionable or have little real chance of successful payback.

Only the board is really in a position to take the first steps toward scam-proofing an organization. The first step, not surprisingly, is to adopt sound investment policies. The second step is even more important. That is to ask the following question of every transaction in which the organization is writing a check: Do we or do we not expect to get our money back? Are we, in other words, making an investment or making a grant? If we are making an investment, then most of the time merely following established investment policies will be sufficient to avoid scams. But in every case, part of the "bait" will be an opportunity that appears too good to be true.

PRACTICAL OBSERVATION 13
IT REALLY IS TOO GOOD TO BE TRUE

The two most widely publicized scams of recent years were the Foundation for New Era of Philanthropy, run by a man named John Bennett out of Philadelphia and the more recent fraudulent hedge fund run by Bernard Madoff in New York. On the face of it, the two schemes were quite different.

The New Era for Philanthropy was promoted as a program of matching grants. Bennett told his victims he had a wealthy donor who would match donations made to worthy organizations. To prove their worthiness, however, organizations had to demonstrate their own capacity by putting funds into an escrow account for one year, at the end of which time those funds and the matching grant would be returned. This scheme was heavily promoted among many faith-based charities and ultimately snared a great many large and well-known organizations. As the first participants received their matching grants, the word spread and soon many, many groups were lining up to apply for matching grants.

Bernard Madoff, on the other hand, ran a hedge fund built with money Madoff raised, initially, through his vast personal connections. The fund's unique appeal was its ability to generate modest steady gains across all market cycles, year in and year out, with nary a blip or down month, let alone down quarter or a down year. As the first participants received reports of their steady returns, many, many groups lined up to invest funds with Madoff.

Both operations were Ponzi schemes in which the earlier participants received distributions with money taken from later investors or contributors. The other thing that they both shared in common was that they were too good to be true. In both instances, there were very cautious people who looked at the opportunity, just didn't trust what they saw, and walked away. If something appears too good to be true, it almost always is. Just walk away.

The other thing that only a board can really do is create an organizational atmosphere of patience and caution, beginning with a board declaration that the directors bear the ultimate responsibility for the financial health of the organization. The board declares, in essence, **we** are ultimately responsible for our financial well-being and in that regard, **we** are there to assist the executives and staff in raising the funds to support the vital work of their nonprofit. Most nonprofit executives I know would consider that a wonderful blessing.

SPENDING POLICY

Spending policy is largely, but not exclusively, an issue that applies to endowments and other long-term funds. There are two related questions:

1. How much can we or should we spend?

2. Are there any restrictions on the source of funds we use for spending?

In the old prudent-man world (see Chapter 3), it was generally acceptable to "spend the income." Dividends and interest could be spent, but capital gains needed to be retained. Thus, the only way to increase spending was to increase earnings, either by investing in higher yielding instruments or by changing the overall asset allocation to increase the percentage of funds held in yield-generating instruments. Ironically, such changes could actually increase portfolio risks.

With the advent of the prudent-investor concept and its emphasis on investing for total return, it is no longer necessary to restrict spending to income from a strictly legal perspective. There may, of course, still be circumstances in which spending is constrained by the terms of a specific instrument or other legal requirement, but when that is not the case, spending policy should be based on a fund's net asset value and not its income.

This is an area in which the Uniform Prudent Management of Institutional Funds Act has adopted new, explicit language for the sake of updating and clarifying the understanding of permissible spending.

The Act begins with the assertion that

> An institution may appropriate for expenditure or accumulate so much of an endowment fund as the institution determines is prudent for the uses, benefits, purposes, and duration for which the endowment fund is established.

The basic rule, in other words, is that the organization may spend whatever is prudent. More on that in a moment. In a later section, the act deals with the whole notion of only spending the income by declaring as follows:

> (c) Terms in a gift instrument designating a gift as an endowment, or a direction or authorization in the gift instrument to use only "income", "interest", "dividends", or "rents, issues, or profits", or "to preserve the principal intact", or words of similar import:
>
> (1) create an endowment fund of permanent duration unless other language in the gift instrument limits the duration or purpose of the fund; and
>
> (2) do not otherwise limit the authority to appropriate for expenditure or accumulate under subsection (a).

Instruments, in other words, that limit spending are now understood to be establishing endowments from which the institution may still base spending on total return as opposed to current income.

That, of course, makes it all the more important to determine what constitutes a prudent amount to spend. To provide guidance there, the Act reads as follows:

> In making a determination to appropriate or accumulate, the institution shall act in good faith, with the care that an ordinarily prudent person in a like position would exercise under similar circumstances, and shall consider, if relevant, the following factors:
>
> (1) the duration and preservation of the endowment fund;
>
> (2) the purposes of the institution and the endowment fund;
>
> (3) general economic conditions;
>
> (4) the possible effect of inflation or deflation;
>
> (5) the expected total return from income and the appreciation of investments;
>
> (6) other resources of the institution; and
>
> (7) the investment policy of the institution.

Perhaps not surprisingly, many of the same concepts and concerns that inform our determination of prudent investing are also allowed to inform our determination of prudent spending. It suggests a unity of approach and thinking that makes a great deal of sense.

Colleges and universities have long led the way in developing a widely-used model for spending endowment funds. While details vary, a common policy is to spend 5 percent of net asset value in quarterly increments on a 36-month (12 quarters) trailing basis. A sample of such a spending policy can be found in Appendix III. The approach is very simple: Take the fund's value at the end of the last 12 quarters, add it up, and divide by 12. You may now spend 1.25 percent of that amount for the quarter which equals 5 percent per year. Three months later you repeat the exercise and spend another 1.25 percent.

What this policy produces is a steady and predictable spending pattern. Large capital gains in one quarter will only increase spending slightly, just as major losses will only lower it slightly. In addition, because markets have trended upward over long periods of time, a spending policy based on trailing values will also tend to lower the amount to be spent. Thus, a 5 percent policy, as calculated above, will turn out, in practice, to produce a slightly lower amount (such as 4.75 percent of the current values).

The UPMIFA acknowledges this aspect of its recommended policy with an optional provision that reads in pertinent part as follows:

(d) The appropriation for expenditure in any year of an amount greater than seven percent of the fair market value of an endowment fund, calculated on the basis of market values determined at least quarterly and averaged over a period of not less than three years immediately preceding the year in which the appropriation for expenditure is made, creates a rebuttable presumption of imprudence.

Under that language it is imprudent to spend more than 7 percent per year, calculated in the trailing quarterly basis described above.

Overall, the new language of the UPMIFA is particularly good news from an investment perspective. A net-asset–value-based spending policy will reduce or eliminate the pressure to "chase yield" by isolating investment policy from spending pressures. Spending will come in a disciplined and predetermined way from all available assets and will not be dependent solely on income. Therefore, investment policy can be established based on overall risk-and-return objectives without having to artificially allocate investment funds to bonds or other fixed-income instruments for the sole purpose of generating income.

Such a policy also makes spending highly predictable. An organization's treasurer, controller, or chief financial officer can make a reasonable estimate of actual spending at the beginning of each year. Even large capital gains or large losses will not have a major impact on budgets and spending.

The final benefit of this approach is that it will often eliminate contentious discussion about spending at the board level. If investment returns are strong, spending will increase — but slowly — and the fund will grow as a result of the retained gains. If losses are incurred, spending will be reduced, but slowly. The organization is thereby insulated from wild swings in spending — and painful decisions having to be made by the board.

CASE STUDY
SPENDING VS. INVESTING

A nonprofit with substantial investments has been spending on programs 5 percent of its invested assets for the last five years. About 25 percent of the investment funds have been restricted by the donor as an endowment for which the corpus may not be spent. Because of a conservative investment strategy, the underlying value of the investments has been relatively unscathed by the market fluctuations since 2000. This year, because of greater demand on the organization's programs, some members of the board advocated increasing the amount of spending from 5 to 8 or 10 percent per year. How did the board go about deciding on this question?

The first issue the board examined was the program needs that were being used to justify an increase in spending. Were they legitimate? Were they immediate? Or could they be postponed or spread out over several years to minimize the financial impact? Were there other ways to pay for the program increases, such as other funding sources, partnering with another organization, or a fee-for-service program?

Ultimately, the board determined that the increased program spending was justified and that there were no funding sources other than assets. They then faced a quandary: how to increase spending from assets without invading the principal of the restricted endowment fund.

Several board members argued for a more aggressive investment strategy that would produce higher returns from which to fund increased programs. Their investment advisor cautioned, however, that this was not a good strategy to follow for the short term. Quick gains in the equity or bond markets — to fund the program increases — would be a most risky and uncertain gamble.

Other board members advocated invading the corpus of the restricted endowment, since the law in their state permitted some limited spending of the principal. However, the board determined that it should honor the original intentions of the donor.

Another board member stated that, with a less conservative investment strategy, increased returns would, in the long run, make up for increased spending out of the

continued on page 56

---

continued from page 55

asset base. However, their investment advisor pointed to studies that have shown that, no matter what a nonprofit's investment strategy, it is virtually impossible to spend more than 5 percent of its assets annually and maintain the underlying value of the fund (net of inflation). And with 25 percent of the assets restricted, it would present even more of a challenge not to quickly erode the other 75 percent. Therefore, even a modest spending increase to 8 or 10 percent could significantly reduce the value of the nonprofit's assets.

After this thorough discussion of options and consequences, the board ultimately decided to resist the pressure for immediate increased spending from the nonprofit's assets. However, it directed its investment committee and advisor to evaluate a more aggressive investment strategy that might produce higher returns, which could fund needed program spending over the next five years. Like an ocean liner, most nonprofits' investments and strategies cannot and should not "turn on a dime." This board finally concluded that a slow-and-steady approach was the best course for it to follow.

CONFLICTS OF INTEREST

Laws concerning nonprofit conflicts of interest are intended to provide a governance structure for defining, and in a sense, allowing such conflicts. Within certain constraints, board members are permitted to lend money to, provide services to, sell property to, and participate in joint ventures with charitable organizations on whose boards they serve.

But when it comes to investing the funds of a nonprofit, board members serve themselves and their organizations best by entirely avoiding any conflict, or appearance of conflict, when possible. Consequently, if you own or work for a professional investment company, the best approach is to not involve your company in providing investment management services to a nonprofit on whose board you serve — even if you are not profiting from those services.

The unique problem of the investment management conflict of interest is that it can adversely impact the board's ability to supervise. It is much more difficult for a board or investment committee to do that job adequately if one of its members is performing the underlying service. Everyone's natural tendency is to withhold criticism or probing questions from people who are otherwise friends and colleagues. Therefore, the best, simplest, and least burdensome approach with regard to investment management is simply to avoid any potential for conflict of interest. Choose a position: Be a service provider or be a director, but do not try to sit on both sides of the table.

Sometimes, however, particularly for small organizations, avoiding the conflict completely is not possible. For some, their board member/investment manager is so committed to the organization that no one can even imagine not having that person fill both roles. And in fairness to those in that situation, most state conflict-of-interest laws permit a board member to recuse himself from voting and thereby avoid a direct conflict when providing services. In that case, it is very important that all parties carefully deal with the potential conflict of interest ahead of time by (1) clearly disclosing the potential conflict to the board, (2) obtaining the board's formal consent, and (3) consistently excusing the member concerned from any voting on investment matters. In addition, the board member/investment manager should not serve on the investment committee, if there is one.

Investment professionals who are not providing services should otherwise be welcome to sit on a board and/or investment committee in order to provide their specialized knowledge and unique viewpoints to the other board members. Such professionals should then be guided by the same conflict-of-interest rules that apply to all members of the board. When the occasion does arise for a professional to influence decisions that would benefit her company or herself personally (such as approving an investment that her company is promoting), then complete disclosure and abstention from participation — in writing, discussion, or voting — should be the guiding principle for one and all.

PRACTICAL OBSERVATION 14
IT'S THE PERFECTLY LEGAL CONFLICTS THAT WEAR YOU OUT

A common, difficult phone call for investment officers begins with someone saying, "I have a friend in the investment business who would like to talk to you about helping our organization. He's a really good supporter of ours and a terrific guy." These calls often come from development officers (people in charge of fundraising), who are hoping the business relationship will lead to donations. When I get such calls, my initial response depends in part on whether I am fully caffeinated by that point in the day. Completely awake I will usually say, "Great, have him give me a call." Otherwise, in a too-honest moment I may say, "That's fine. Just make sure he knows we won't be hiring him so long as the earth is in orbit around the sun."

Here's the story behind my peevishness. More often than not, the "friend in the investment business" doesn't want to "help the ministry," he wants to manage some of the organization's money. While that may or may not be helpful, he is a prospective service provider, not a donor. To the extent he is trying to look or act like a donor, he is essentially creating a soft form of conflict of interest that will do nothing but cause problems on down the road.

The essence of prudent investment behavior is objective analysis and dispassionate implementation. In that regard, it's a bit like going to war. You want mission-oriented troops who will follow orders. Friends, of the type described above, all want to be generals. Their first goal is to get some assets to manage. Their second goal is to get more assets to manage. There are no third goals.

Consequently, when people with close, personal ties to an organization become service providers, the personal relationships have a tendency to compromise future decisions. If we hire a friend and the friend doesn't perform well, can we fire him? Perhaps. But not in the same, dispassionate, matter-of-fact way we would with people who do not have such ties. You order troops into battle; you ask a general if this is a good time to fight.

Consequently, even with all the good will in the world, the consultant or chief investment officer will say, "No," most of the time. Since no one likes to be told, "No," I am always concerned about the possible impact of these calls. It is a situation in which an introduction can lead to hurt feelings and actually make the fundraising task more difficult.

All of that said, I'm not naïve to enough to think that we can run our organizations without referrals from friends and acquaintances. Personal relationships are an important part of any business. So these introductions will always occur and need to be managed. How do we do that?

First, it helps when folks with fundraising responsibilities understand the realities of investment management. Development officers have a very tough job and work hard to build relationships with prospective donors. When people in that role realize that much of the time an organization cannot hire their potential donor-advisor-friend, then everyone can work together to manage expectations. Most important, development officers need to discuss potential referrals with their investment officer or consultant before promising an introduction to the advisor. That step alone will eliminate 95 percent of the problems.

Second, when making an introduction, be as clear as possible about the authority of your investment team. When an insider tells a prospective service provider, "Bob is in charge of these decisions, and I have no pull, so don't get your hopes up," he is essentially saying, "Bob is the general, and he will hire you only if he needs your type of soldier." That makes the entire conversation much easier and, ironically, also makes it easier for me to shift into schmooze mode and try to help build the relationship.

Ultimately, the best of all possible worlds is to disassociate investment service providers from fundraising as much as possible. Hire workers to work. Recruit donors based on the value of your mission and ministry. Stay away from the seemingly easy path of courting donors by hiring them, or their friends, to provide services. In my experience, that rarely works out very well.

? ACTION QUESTIONS

1. Do we have unambiguous gift-acceptance policies?

2. Do we have a set of roles and responsibilities for our investment committee? Are they well understood and carried out appropriately?

3. What is our approach to socially-responsible investing?

4. Can we justify our spending policy in terms of meeting the needs of today and remaining sustainable in the future?

5. Do we have a solid conflict-of-interest policy to eliminate private agendas?

CHAPTER 5
GETTING HELP

There are lots of ways to invest your money, even after you've more or less decided where it should go. To put money into the U.S. stock market, for example, you can buy an index fund, invest through a mutual fund, or hire an investment manager to create a customized portfolio. Each approach has its pros and cons. When it comes to getting help, however, the rich variety of investment options makes it harder to find the help that's right for you. Different types of advisors tend to use, or to be tied to, different investment tools.

To understand the kinds of help available, we will first look at the component tasks of investment management and the different methods of getting those tasks done. We will also clarify the relationships between the tasks and the different types of service providers. Finally, we will consider the connection between the size of our holdings and the types of help we can expect.

As you begin putting your knowledge of investing into practice, my strong prejudice is that you want someone who can act as an overall consultant — someone who understands the big picture, with all its parts. However, "consultant" does not refer to any particular type of license, nor to any particular investment technique. It is a functional role, not a formal classification. Consequently, the task of finding the right consultant can be daunting. We will end this chapter with some remarks on that topic.

INVESTMENT TASKS AND SERVICE PROVIDERS

The investment management process can be broken down into five steps:

1. Decide on asset allocation.

2. Select specific investments (e.g., stocks, bonds, and other instruments).

3. Purchase and sell investments (i.e., securities brokerage).

4. Maintain custody of the assets.

5. Report on performance.

Whatever combination of service providers and investment techniques you decide to use, you must cover all five functions. Today we can achieve that result in a number of different ways, thanks largely to the proliferation of investment structures and investment technology over the past 30 years.

It is possible to get all five functions in one package. When you buy into a mutual fund, for example, the fund's advisor selects the securities and then directs the trades through one or more brokers. If the fund company also offers an asset allocation service, maintains custody of the shares, and provides a performance report, then the mutual fund effectively provides all five functions. This is a very efficient option for smaller-scale investing, since mutual funds typically accept investments as low as $1,000. Nonprofit organizations commonly use mutual funds when total assets under management are less than $1 million.

A so-called wrap account can also provide all five investment functions. In this arrangement, a major brokerage house charges a single, asset-based fee to provide custody and trading functions, plus access to third-party investment management services. Annual fees are graduated, with the highest percentage charged on the smallest accounts (typically under $100,000) and rates decreasing as the assets under management increase. In addition to investment selection and trading services, most programs provide multiclass asset allocation services and performance reporting as part of the package. Nonprofit organizations commonly use wrap programs when total assets under management range from $5 million to $50 million or more.

For very large nonprofits, with at least $100 million under management, there comes a point where it is more cost-effective to buy the various services separately. Thus, larger organizations can retain a consultant to provide asset allocation and performance reporting, and at the same time they can contract directly with one or more investment advisors for investment selection, direct the advisors to trade through particular brokers, and set up asset custody at one of many large banks. This practice is the norm in the world of billion-dollar endowments.

The primary service providers for the five core investment functions are securities brokers, generally referred to broker/dealers; banks and trust companies; and registered investment advisors, sometimes called investment managers. For the most part, these groups reflect particular licensing structures under federal and state securities laws. Consequently, when nontraditional providers, such as insurance companies, attorneys, accountants, or financial planners, provide any of these services, they are commonly doing so either as registered investment advisors or through brokerage subsidiaries or affiliates.

Within the five functional areas, only broker/dealers can actually trade stocks and bonds on exchanges, and only banks, trust companies, or broker/dealers typically provide custody. All of the other functions, however — asset allocation, investment selection, and performance reporting — are typically provided both by registered investment advisors and by the broker/dealers and banks, acting in that same capacity. This overlap of services is probably the single biggest source of confusion about who does what.

PASSIVE STRUCTURES VS. ACTIVE ADVISORS

The arrangements described thus far involve some form of active management. Whether the money is in a mutual fund or a separately managed account, someone, typically a registered investment advisor, is trying to add value by selecting investments. An alternative is so-called passive investing, by which investors hold interests in an entire market or market segment through an index fund or an exchange-traded fund. Such funds typically track a specific index, such as the S&P 500. By dispensing with time-consuming research and the transaction costs of frequent trading, index funds gain a cost advantage over actively managed ones. Many index funds have internal costs and fees below 0.5 percent. Fees in traditional, actively managed mutual funds average 1.5 percent or more, in addition to transaction costs.

Index fund proponents often argue that because of this cost difference, active managers do not, and most likely cannot, reliably outperform index funds. And indeed, the record of active advisors versus index funds is mixed, at best. One study that carefully compared active and passive mutual funds arrived at the following conclusion:

> We find that, on average, index funds outperform actively managed funds for most equity and all bond fund categories on both a before-tax and after-tax basis. However, actively managed Small Company Equity (SCE) funds and International Stock (IS) funds significantly outperform the index over most of the study period. Managers of these funds appear to be able to invest to take advantage of mispricing in these presumably less efficient markets.[5]

This does not mean that you should stay away from actively managed funds. It does mean that you should think about your goals and consider how active management will help you reach them. Active managers are more likely to outperform the indices in lessser-developed or less-liquid markets than in large-capitalization markets like those represented by the S&P 500. But remember, also, that there can be reasons other than fund performance for using active managers. Separately managed accounts are ideal for minimizing the income tax impacts of investments. Even in the charitable world, some assets, such as those held in charitable remainder trusts, benefit from tax-efficient management. In addition, socially- or morally-based investment restrictions create a need for some sort of active management.

Finally, it is interesting to note that today many of the largest and most sophisticated investment operations in the world use a mix of active and passive investment strategies for the publicly traded portion of their portfolios. In the debate over active versus passive strategies, we may be asking the wrong question (just as we were on the matter of costs in Practical Observation 9, back in Chapter 3). The real question is "What is the best way for us to invest our funds in this particular asset class and within the context of our overall allocation?"

---

[5] Fortin, Rich and Stuart Michelson, "Indexing Versus Active Mutual Fund Management." *Journal of Financial Planning,* September 2002.

PRACTICAL OBSERVATION 15
WHAT A MANAGER CAN DO DEPENDS IN PART ON WHAT HE IS TOLD TO DO

For many years, and continuing to this day, the institutional investment model is to give managers very narrow mandates. The common name for this approach is "hiring experts." We might, for example, hire a Large-Cap Value Manager and ask him to outperform the S&P 500 value index. The problem is that such mandates essentially force managers to closely follow the index. Why is that a problem?

With an index type mandate, the manager must first diversify across many shares, typically at least 40 or 50, in a mix that more or less reflects the sector weightings of the index. So if the index holds 30 percent bank shares, the manager will typically hold anywhere from 20 to 40 percent bank shares. And here's the point: The bank share allocation in that portfolio will not be zero, even if the manager thinks bank shares are a horrible investment.

It follows that the manager has to try to beat the index by picking the top stocks in each category. In my opinion, that is a very difficult task. Our disappointment with active-manager returns in comparison to passive structures, such as index funds, may therefore be tied to the fact that the managers are often forced to track the index anyway. If you have to be just like an index *and* you have a 2 or 3 percent greater annual cost structure, how can you really hope to outperform? Probably you can't.

One active manager I have used and appreciated for many years has run a global, value-oriented mutual fund for the past three decades. The manager's mandate, significantly, is very broad, allowing the fund to buy — or, more important, not buy — shares anywhere in the world. When, in the past, the manager did not like market conditions or could not find shares that met the fund's investment criteria, they sat in cash. As a result of their discipline, their relative performance has been very good, particularly during severely down markets. The fund isn't for everyone, of course — no fund is. But it illustrates an approach in which the manager has the potential to actually add value. In my opinion, managers can only add value if they have the necessary freedom.

The point is that our structures must suit our goals. If we seek S&P 500 returns for part of our portfolio, we might as well use the very inexpensive index funds. If we want exposure to small-company stocks in Asia, then I'm inclined to use a manager with people on the ground and expertise in the area and the freedom to choose investments without rigid adherence to an index. In every case, we are attempting to match the management tool to the task.

PRICING OF SERVICES

In the pricing of investment services, there aren't any clear-cut break points based on asset size that dictate using one structure over another. While mutual funds, for example, are generally expensive from an institutional perspective, today many fund companies offer institutional share classes on which the mutual fund provider has dramatically lowered fees in exchange for much larger minimum investments.

In addition, there are sometimes pricing anomalies that can make an investment structure designed for one market attractive in another. The major brokerage firms' wrap-fee programs are an example. These programs were designed for the retail market, meaning individual investors with assets, typically, in the $100,000 to $1 million range. The fees off the rate sheets are very high, starting at 3 percent, typically, on the first dollars. At that, they can be more expensive than mutual funds.

However, wrap-fee programs have two important features. First, fees are negotiable. Brokers can and do reduce their fees all the time. Second, at least in the programs with which I am familiar, the people designing the fee schedules never really expected very many $10 million-plus accounts. So those fees can be quite modest, with all-in charges of less than 1 percent on equity and balanced accounts. At that level, it can make a lot of sense to use a "retail" product for your "institutional" investing.

Ultimately, it is important to know what you are being charged and how the fees are calculated. But don't start there. Start with a search for whichever fund, index, advisor or ETF appears to be the best at providing exposure to the asset class in which you want to invest. Then figure out what it will cost you to use that structure in comparison to the other choices. Fees matter, but an excessive focus on fees can easily become the tail wagging the dog.

THE IMPORTANCE AND ROLE OF A CONSULTANT

The optimal combination of investment management service providers depends on the type and size of your manageable funds and the sophistication of your investment committee and staff. As an organization's funds increase in size, the continuum of service options grows from (typically) all-in-one service providers to specialized providers for every component. But no matter which investment structure or combination of services an organization selects, someone really needs to act as an overall strategist and advisor. The world of very large institutional accounts has long used so-called consultants to fill this role. They may be registered investment advisors, affiliates of securities brokers, or, occasionally, bankers. The only difference for smaller nonprofits is that (largely for cost reasons) the "consultant" might be your broker or your registered investment advisor and not a separately retained, freestanding advisor.

Using an advisor as a consultant provides the board or investment committee with a degree of independent oversight, accountability, and performance reporting. Such a consultant can also provide other valuable services: evaluating potential gifts of equities or bonds; attending board and committee meetings to explain investment actions, options, and strategies; and even meeting with donors and others to explain an organization's investment policies and approach. At the end of the day, it can be wonderful having such help.

The best way to start your search for advisors is to contact the executives of comparably sized organizations in your area and ask for a recommendation. Ask if they have a principal advisor or consultant, whether they have separate brokerage and custodial relationships, and how the actual investments are being implemented (e.g., funds, separately managed accounts, or both). Solicit their comments on the advisors they are using, and you will soon have a list of candidates to interview.

Be sure you understand exactly how each service provider is compensated. A potential advisor should be able to explain in a single, cogent sentence how he will be remunerated for the work he does. Most advisors today are compensated on a fee-for-service basis, typically (but not always) expressed as a percentage of assets under management. (In the multi-billion-dollar pension plan world, fixed-dollar consulting relationships become more common.) If you understand how and when each provider is compensated, you will be a better judge of any compensation bias that might be contained in the advisor's recommendations.

At the end of this process, you should have identified someone to act as the nonprofit's consultant, charged with the task of advising the chief financial officer, the investment committee, and the full board on asset allocation, manager or fund selection, and performance reporting. As we have seen, this service is essential for proper supervision. It can also be a wonderful comfort for board members not to face the complex world of investments alone.

ACTION QUESTIONS

1. What structure or combination of services seems most attractive to us, given the size and complexity of our funds?

2. Do we have a clear idea of the cost of our current investment program?

3. Have we gathered the information we need to search for a consultant in a disciplined process?

CHAPTER 6
21ST CENTURY INVESTMENT ISSUES

At the start of the 21st century, several worldwide trends are shaping the investment environment. Nonprofit board members need to know about

- globalization
- the growing role of alternative investments
- the dangers of "fiat" currencies

GLOBALIZATION

Normally I hesitate to talk about trends, since that's only half a step removed from making predictions. But globalization is an essential context for any discussion of current investment issues. For centuries, kings and countries erected barriers to the exchange and sale of goods from the outside. Sometimes enacted to raise tax revenue, sometimes to protect local industries, the barriers all had the same effect: to inhibit trade. But since the end of World War II, nations and international organizations have worked steadily and systematically to eliminate those barriers.

The assault on trade barriers has stepped up dramatically in recent years:

- NAFTA (the North American Free Trade Agreement) now largely allows the free flow of goods between the United States, Mexico, and Canada.

- The European Union (EU) has largely eliminated trade barriers among its member nations and is actively engaged in reducing trade and agricultural barriers with other regions of the world. The EU has also introduced a new currency, the euro, which is vying with the dollar to become the world's reserve currency.

- The General Agreement on Tariffs and Trade (GATT) is the largest and most comprehensive trade agreement in the world and, in combination with the World Trade Organization, has standardized trade and negotiated the removal of countless tariffs.

While tariffs, trade restrictions, and domestic subsidies remain in place in many countries, the clear trend is toward a world in which goods and services flow freely between nations. What this means for investors is that there is no longer such a thing as a purely domestic investment. Fifty years ago, it was possible to invest in portfolios of domestic stocks and bonds without giving the rest of the world much thought. The United States had emerged from World War II as the only major nation with its economy intact.

A half-century later, the United States shares economic power with nations around the world. We depend on other nations to buy our products, to sell us low-cost goods and services, and, increasingly, to lend us money. In addition, the extent of globalization and the resulting free and secure flow of capital around the world has effectively removed the disincentives to international investing. Investment capital is increasingly seeking the best returns — wherever in the world those might be found.

To keep pace with these developments, most investors — including nonprofits — must open their portfolios to international investments. Really, this is another type of diversification, which hedges the risks associated with investing only in the United States. One way to invest internationally is direct purchase of foreign equities, although some new dangers, such as currency risks, are thereby introduced into a portfolio. But in this arena, technique is less important than mindset. We simply need to understand that investing is now, unavoidably, an international activity.

ALTERNATIVE INVESTMENTS

In recent years, nonprofits have increasingly turned to so-called alternative investments. These are usually complicated investment structures, often in partnership format, sold as private placements rather than as publicly registered securities. A private placement is a legal sale to a limited group of purchasers, done so as to avoid securities-law requirements associated with selling to the general public. The theory of private-placement exemption from securities laws is that the purchasers are sophisticated parties, able to protect themselves.

Perhaps the best-known type of alternative investment is the hedge fund. The label refers to a broad class of investments with the following characteristics: (1) they are created in partnership (or LLC) format, (2) they are unconstrained by diversification requirements, (3) they are typically free to pursue strategies like short selling — the technique of selling borrowed shares in the expectation that prices will subsequently fall, so that shares can be bought back at a lower price for return to the original lender, (4) the general partner/managers often have their own money invested in the funds, and (5) the managers usually receive performance-based fees. Hedge funds frequently use leverage and are almost always sold as private placements. They tend to be based on particular investment strategies: market-neutral, distressed-securities, convertible-arbitrage, or event-driven, to name just some.

Why should a nonprofit organization consider such a complex investment? One answer is noncorrelation, the term the financial world uses to describe investments that do not respond in the same way to outside economic events. Recall the discussion in Chapter 2 of asset allocation: noncorrelated assets can greatly reduce a portfolio's volatility and thereby improve its risk-adjusted performance over time. As a direct result of being able to sell positions short, being able to make concentrated investments, and not being publicly traded, many hedge funds historically have a low degree of correlation to the broad market of publicly traded securities.

However, noncorrelation is only part of the story. After all, certain other asset classes, including cash and bonds (particularly short- to mid-term bonds), have an even lower correlation to equities and for that reason have long been used to reduce risk in portfolios. But cash and bonds also produce significantly lower total returns (historically) than hedge funds and some other alternative investments. The allure of hedge funds is the prospect of low correlation with reasonable returns as a tool for reducing broad market risk. Let's examine whether or not that in fact worked in recent years.

The chart below compares the S&P 500 to a broad fund-of-funds index for the period from October 2007, near the beginning of the public awareness of the credit crisis, through March of 2009. What is immediately obvious is that the hedge funds, while declining in value by approximately 23 percent, still far outperformed the S&P 500, which lost nearly half its value during the same period.

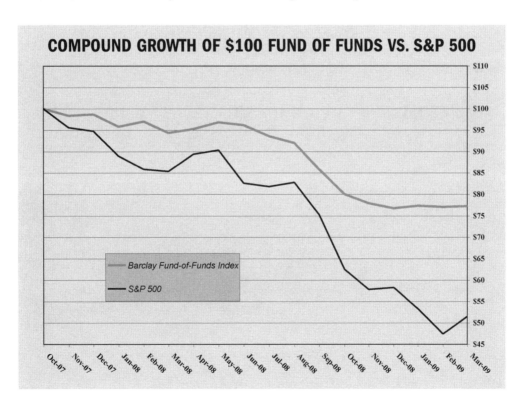

The ability of hedge funds to earn returns in poor markets, or this case to lose less in a catastrophic market, is due to their use of techniques such as short selling. Their potential to add protection against macroeconomic trends is a risk-reduction reason for adding such investments to a portfolio.

WEAKNESSES OF THE REGULATED INVESTMENT WORLD

An interesting additional reason to consider alternative investments is, ironically, the lack of a direct correlation between government regulation and investment safety. Even if we accept as a given that there is some value in government regulation generally, that value does not necessarily translate into real-life protection of investors against losses. In point of fact, the nation's fundamental securities regulations, meaning the laws covering the sale of stocks and bonds, are not really focused on investment safety at all. When, for example, the Securities and Exchange Commission (SEC) allows a company to sell publicly-traded stock, the soundness of the investment is not itself a regulatory issue. Rather, the entire focus is on disclosure of all the material facts and circumstances, including risk factors, that collectively describe the investment. **Consequently, there is no direct link between government regulation of an investment and its safety.**

Consider the following chart. It shows the recent price performance of Citibank, the largest bank in the U.S.; AIG, the country's largest insurance company; and Fannie Mae and Freddie Mac, the country's largest mortgage lenders. By early 2009, all of these gigantic, publicly regulated entities were in or near bankruptcy, having together destroyed roughly $600 billion of shareholder equity.

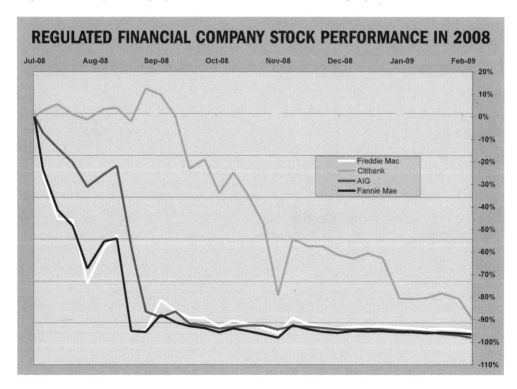

Here's the point: These are (or were) also among the most highly regulated companies in the United States. Fannie Mae and Freddie Mac even had a regulator, the Office of Federal Housing Enterprise Oversight, just for them. With the approval of this regulator (and the active support of Congress), they leveraged themselves more than 100-to-1. Modest loan losses then triggered massive failure. I wish it were otherwise, but regulation means very little in terms of ensuring the safety of investments.

CHECKS AND BALANCES IN THE HEDGE FUND WORLD

If government regulation is inadequate to protect investments, it does not follow that lack of regulation means things are safe. Obviously (very obviously), there are dangerous investments in the lightly regulated hedge fund world. But it is important to understand that hedge funds are subject to meaningful checks and balances.

Among the more important:

1. Most hedge fund managers have a majority of their own net worth invested in their funds. Part of the problem with the world of regulated Wall Street is that executive officers are paid to take risks with other people's money. The hedge fund approach, in which the manager has his or her own funds at risk with the investors', is much to be preferred.

2. Many hedge funds are regularly audited by major accounting firms.

3. Many hedge funds have banking relationships with major global banks, which routinely verify the strength of the hedge funds' operating systems and the validity of their assets.

4. Some fund-of-fund managers independently perform and maintain due diligence on the funds in which they invest.

5. The actual hedge fund assets are typically held at major global banks.

6. In the institutional world — the world of ERISA Pension Plan investors and U.S. nonprofit investors — hedge funds typically retain independent third-party administrators to provide accounting and record-keeping services.

7. Many hedge fund managers are actually modestly regulated because they are registered investment advisors, subject to supervision by the SEC.

None of these items on its own guarantees the safety of invested funds, but together they establish a well-understood path by which investors can usually avoid most fraudulent transactions. The number one statement made by those who lost money in the Madoff scandal is that they, or their intermediaries, failed to perform proper due diligence. The fact is, many who did due diligence on Madoff "smelled a rat" and declined to invest. (See references to details of the scandal in the Suggested Resources.)

For all of that, hedge funds and other alternative investments (such as private equity investments and "managed futures") are not for the faint of heart and not to be used lightly. Their illiquidity greatly restricts the percentage of any portfolio that can be allocated to such instruments and their complexity virtually mandates the use of a specialized investment advisor or consultant. As discussed in our final Practical Observation, complexity alone is a reason to be wary.

Finally, most alternative investment programs have significant buy-in minimums that will prevent nonprofits with small investment funds from participating. But nonprofits with substantial, long-term funds in endowments, pension plans, or other assets with similar time horizons should consider alternative investments as part of their portfolios. With caution and in appropriate amounts, these tools have the potential for reducing portfolio risks. Appendix II includes a further discussion of the relevant due diligence issues.

PRACTICAL OBSERVATION 17
BEWARE OF COMPLEXITY[6]

Although I can now find plenty to read online, I still prefer reading a real book, made of ink and paper. For many of the same reasons, I like working with hand tools. Power tools and computers have their place, but I enjoy the quaint reliability and simplicity of the older instruments.

There is also a kind of safety in these less-complicated tools. I know several men who have lost fingers using table saws, but I've yet to meet anyone who severed a digit with a hand saw. The true beauty of the older instruments is that they are simple to understand and safe to use. When I pick up a hand saw, I know what to expect, and my ability to cut things is limited by my strength and endurance. In a very real sense, the tool matches my abilities.

In the first decade of this century, some of the world's largest banks and financial institutions lost hundreds of billions of dollars by investing in instruments too powerful for them to control and too complicated for them to understand. These structures, known by names like Collateralized Mortgage Obligations (CMOs), Collateralized Debt Obligations (CDOs), and Credit Default Swaps (CDS) — all derive their values from combinations of mortgages or other debts.

In the olden days, banks' ability to lend was strongly constrained by the funds they had on deposit. Their ability to grow their business was thus limited by their ability to attract funds from depositors, and their leverage was limited by the amount of equity (so-called Tier 1 Capital) they were required to maintain. They made hand-saw loans, if you will, that were limited by the strength of the financial institution.

[6] This Practical Observation was first published in the National Christian Foundation's *Gathering Newsletter* in December 2007 and is used here with permission.

But in the early 1980s, Wall Street investment bankers became power tool salesmen by designing the structures just described and selling them to investors for a fee. The bankers thought that they had died and gone to heaven. They could now make loans to their hearts' content, charge origination fees, sell the loans into securitization vehicles, get their money back, and then do it all over again. The growth of their business was no longer limited by their own financial strength, only by their ability to sell. The CMOs and CDOs became the table saws of the financial tool shop.

Wall Street was equally delighted. Here was a whole new source of very substantial fees for packaging and selling securities. On the theory that if a little power is great, more is better, Wall Street quickly added complexity and leverage to the mix. Complexity came from cutting the offerings into tranches (French for "slice"), each with a different set of rights that made some tranches relatively safer than others. Incredibly, the "safest" tranches, those with the first right to income from the underlying loans, were soon granted AAA ratings, even though the underlying assets were still very, very risky. Obviously, the AAA paper was easier for Wall Street to sell than other, lower-rated paper.

Leverage spread and grew just as quickly, as hedge funds, the banks themselves, and a wide range of financial intermediaries began borrowing to invest in these new-fangled securities. The details of the financing structures are too mind-boggling to describe, but suffice it to say that there are now entities such as "Synthetic Collateralized Debt Obligations" that have borrowed money solely to purchase assets in other CMOs and CDOs. This is roughly equivalent to using the engines off a 747 to run our table saw.

So long as everything was going well, the financial super saws promised short paths to huge profits. But when defaults in subprime mortgages caused the whole structure to totter, those same high-powered tools started lopping off financial digits, sometimes nine at a time. The leverage that fueled the growth of the mortgage-backed securities industry now amplified the catastrophe. And the complexity of the instruments, which included the fact that most of these securities were not publicly traded, led to an incredible problem: No one knew what they were really worth. The banks ended up with an arm caught in a financial table saw and no idea how to turn the thing off.

What is the lesson in all this for ordinary people who are trying to supervise the investment of charitable funds? Just this: It's OK to avoid investing in things we do not understand, just because we don't understand them. It's OK, in fact, to be the only one you know who's not using a table saw, just because the thing scares you. Humility is a wonderful investment management tool.

THE DANGERS OF FIAT CURRENCIES

In investing there is probably nothing more difficult to deal with, nor to anticipate, than changes in currency value.

Imagine a world in which gravity, for whatever reasons, doubles. You go to bed weighing 180 pounds and wake up weighing 360 pounds but with your muscle mass unchanged. Your 18-pound poodle tries to jump on your lap and hits your knees. All four tires on your car are flat. You get the picture. No amount of working out and looking after your home can really prepare you for a world in which the weight of everything has suddenly doubled. Changes in currency values are like that.

Today, virtually every country in the world uses fiat currency, which is currency whose value is not anchored to a hard asset. For centuries, many major currencies were convertible, at the holder's request, into gold. But the United States abandoned the gold standard in 1971, as have virtually all other nations in the world, either before or since. Even the Swiss, in May of 2000, abandoned their version of the gold standard, which up until that time had required the government to maintain an amount of gold equal to 40 percent of the value of Swiss francs in circulation.

The danger of fiat currencies isn't literally that they are not backed by gold. Rather, the danger comes from the *reasons* why governments have been abandoning the gold standard. *The absence of such a standard makes it much easier to devalue the currency which, frequently, is the easiest way out of debts or other problems.*

Suppose that after years of borrowing to finance its operations, a country has a hard time bringing in enough tax revenue to make payments on the debt and cover ongoing expenses. What to do? The painful response is to cut government spending and wait for the economy and the resulting tax revenues to grow over time. But what if you control the amount of money outstanding? What if, in effect, you can just print more? If you do that, you can easily pay your debts. However, the flood of new bills drives the value of the currency down — sharply down and sometimes far, far down. In Germany in the 1930s, Mexico in the 1970s, Russia in the 1990s, and Zimbabwe in the 2000s, the currency became effectively worthless. That's the worst-case outcome of currency risk with a fiat currency.

In investing, we lower our exposure to currency risk by making sure our portfolio allocations include so-called hard assets: real estate, oil and gas, timber, commodities (wheat, corn, heating oil, etc.), and gold. Today investors can take positions in all of these, through securities designed for that purpose. There are, for example, exchange-traded funds (ETFs) that hold commodities futures, or proxies for commodities futures, and very closely track the price behavior of a basket of particular commodities. Similarly, there are ETFs that literally own gold bullion and therefore track its price.

Such hedges against potential currency debasement come with their own sets of challenges. At a minimum, however, we need to take account of currency risk. It may prove to be one of the more daunting problems we face as investors in the 21st century.

ACTION QUESTIONS

1. Do our investment policies and portfolios take adequate account of the benefits and risks of globalization and international investing?

2. Have we formulated policies for allowing or restricting alternative investments?

3. Are there steps we can or should take to reduce our currency and/or inflation risk?

4. Do we understand the things in which we have invested, or are we inadvertently taking complexity risk?

CONCLUSION

We end by briefly considering what to do, as directors and supervisors, when things don't work out as we had hoped. There is never a greater need for leadership than in times of crisis. And there is never a better opportunity to act lovingly and hopefully as we look to the future. In recent years, the investment world has been a wonderful place to practice such virtues!

WHAT TO DO WHEN THE WHEELS FALL OFF THE BUS

Sometimes, no matter how careful we are, things turn out badly. In the investment world that usually means our organization has just incurred larger losses investing than we ever thought possible. This leads to the logical question, "Now what?" As it turns out, there are some very practical steps we can take.

The first step is to reassess our tolerance for risk. This might seem like a backward-looking exercise, but it is not. If, as you review a severely underperforming portfolio, you find that the losses you incurred are within the range you anticipated as a worst-case scenario, then your asset-allocation and risk-management decisions were probably correct. If, on the other hand, you are kicking yourself over the size of the losses and now admit they were greater than you could stomach, then recognize that your asset allocation and other risk-management strategies were inadequate. In that case, start over. Ask, once again: Given where you are today and given your future needs, how much downside risk can you accept? That then becomes a critical data point for all future investment decisions, and one of the few data points a good consultant will need to help you build new portfolios.

Next, again root out hidden risks, including hidden leverage. Leverage can kill you. Warren Buffet, in an interview about the credit crisis, said, "Leverage [is] the only way a smart guy can go broke." It is too true. But leverage is everywhere in the world today — explicitly in many, many closed-end mutual funds and hedge funds, and tacitly lurking on the balance sheets of many companies. In some industries, such as banking, it is baked into the regulatory framework. It takes a real effort to find solid, unleveraged investments.

Also, realize that sometimes we are the problem. Our desire for large returns can drive us to seek leveraged investments. A great many hedge funds, for example, posted stunningly large numbers in up markets by leveraging their market exposure. With underlying assets growing at 8 percent, three-to-one leverage on low-cost loans might turn the overall return into 20 percent. Who wouldn't want that? Unfortunately, 3-to-1 leverage can also turn a 25-percent loss into a 75-percent one, which is fatal. Seeking extraordinary returns sometimes makes us vulnerable to inappropriate risks.

The final step is to rebalance our portfolios. Those who maintain their course in tough markets will invariably rebalance to target asset allocations. What does that mean? It means that even after large losses, you may end up being a buyer of equities! What?! Yes, a buyer. Here's why. Suppose your foundation had previously decided to allocate 40 percent to traditional equities, 40 percent to hard assets and hedge funds, and 20 percent to fixed income. After a bad stretch in the stock market, that 40-percent allocation to equities is down to 30 percent or even less. If you have reviewed your asset allocation and determined that (1) the assets chosen are appropriate for today's environment, looking forward, and that (2) it properly balances your risk tolerance and your growth goals, then you should in fact buy to bring the allocations back to your targets. The benefit of this discipline is that it gives you a reason to buy when prices are potentially very low and certainly lower than they were.

LOOK HOPEFULLY TO THE FUTURE

As we saw early in this book, we can't "not invest." Our need to protect our assets against inflation and to secure income for present obligations and future projects does not go away. As much as we might like to stop the world and get off, it's not an option. What we can do, however, is face the future with hope.

Besides helping us get on with the business at hand, a hopeful attitude also frees us to not be unduly critical of those who serve. I know many, many people in the investment management world. A few, near the top, are arrogant, selfish, and dangerous. But the vast majority, including all of the advisors with whom we work, are concerned about their clients and trying at all times to do a good job. When things go wrong, money wasn't lost for lack of effort. Rather, the advisors were doing their best, but their best was overwhelmed by forces they could not necessarily control. Hopeful people can afford to be kind in their dealings with others.

Remember, finally, what hasn't been lost or destroyed in an economic crisis or a stock market decline. Most of the time, we have only lost money. Typically our people are all alive and well; our means of production — roads, bridges, trucks, trains, factories, and fields — are in place, undamaged and functioning; and the vast majority of the nations in the world with whom we trade are at peace. We have much for which to be thankful and much to give us hope.

As a board member of a nonprofit organization, you are charged with supervising the investment of your organization's assets. The thread that runs through this book is the belief that average people — men and women who are not investment professionals — can and should provide guidance and oversight to the investment process of the organizations on whose boards they serve. At the end of the day, there is no substitute for the good judgment the average board member can bring to the process. There is also no substitute for the board member who is willing to ask the obvious questions and apply old-fashioned common sense. If you are willing to ask those questions and apply your sound reasoning powers to the answers, you will serve your organization exceptionally well — and help establish a lasting legacy for the future.

APPENDIX I
SAMPLE INVESTMENT POLICIES

Please see the attached CD-ROM for a downloadable and customizable version of the following sample policies.

The following is a basic set of investment policies for a charitable organization. It establishes an investment committee and authorizes the retention of an investment consultant to guide and assist the committee in its work. It then addresses all of the standard investment policy issues. Please note, however, that this form is only a sample and may not be appropriate for any specific organization without significant modifications and additions. In that regard, this particular set of policies is intended to be helpful primarily to smaller organizations and those adopting policies for the first time, as opposed to organizations with larger or well-established investment operations. When drafting policies, you would ideally do so in conjunction with your investment consultant and should always have such policies reviewed by your legal counsel before adoption.

PREAMBLE

It is the policy of the Board of Directors (Board) to treat all assets of the Nonprofit Organization (NPO), including Funds that are legally unrestricted, as if held by NPO in a fiduciary capacity for the sake of accomplishing its mission and purposes. The following investment objectives and directions are to be judged and understood in light of that overall sense of stewardship. In that regard, the basic investment standards shall be those of a prudent investor as articulated in applicable state laws.

INVESTMENT ASSETS

For purposes of these policies, investment assets are those assets of NPO that are available for investment in the public securities markets as stocks, bonds, cash, or cash equivalents, either directly or through intermediate structures. Illiquid assets are described in NPO's Gift Acceptance Policies, and are governed by those rules and not by these investment policies.

SUPERVISION AND DELEGATION

The Board of Directors of NPO has adopted these policies and has formed an Investment Committee, described below, to whom it has delegated authority to supervise NPO investments. The Board reserves to itself the exclusive right to amend or revise these policies.

INVESTMENT COMMITTEE

The Investment Committee ("Committee") consists of the chief financial officer, _____, Board members, and _____ non–board member(s), who serve at the pleasure of the Board. It shall be the responsibility of the Committee to:

1. Supervise the overall implementation of NPO's investment policies by NPO's executive staff and outside advisors;

2. Monitor and evaluate the investment performance of NPO's Funds;

3. Report regularly on NPO investment matters to the Board of Directors;

4. Grant exceptions as permitted in these policies and recommend changes in approved policy, guidelines, and objectives as needed; and,

5. Execute such other duties as may be delegated by the Board of Directors.

Whenever these policies assign specific tasks to the Committee, the policies assume that the actual work will (or may) be performed by NPO's chief financial officer or other designated staff members, subject only to the Committee's overall supervision.

INVESTMENT CONSULTANT, ADVISORS, AND AGENTS

The Committee is specifically authorized to retain one or more investment advisors (Advisors) as well as any administrators, custodians, or other investment service providers required for the proper management of NPO's Funds. The Committee may utilize an Advisor as an investment consultant (the "Consultant") to advise and assist the Committee in the discharge of its duties and responsibilities. In that regard, a Consultant may help the Committee to:

1. Develop and maintain investment policy, asset allocation strategies, risk-based fund objectives, and appropriate investment management structures;

2. Select, monitor, and evaluate Investment Advisors and/or investment entities;

3. Provide and/or review quarterly performance measurement reports and assist the Committee in interpreting the results;

4. Review portfolios and recommend actions, as needed, to maintain proper asset allocations and investment strategies for the objectives of each fund; and,

5. Execute such other duties as may be mutually agreed.

In discharging this authority, the Committee can act in the place and stead of the Board and may receive reports from, pay compensation to, enter into agreements with, and delegate discretionary investment authority to such Advisors. When delegating discretionary investment authority to one or more Advisors, the Committee will establish and follow appropriate procedures for selecting such Advisors and for conveying to each the scope of their authority, the organization's expectations, and the requirement of full compliance with these Policies.

OBJECTIVES

NPO's primary investment objective is to preserve and protect its assets, by earning a total return for each category of assets (a "Fund"), which is appropriate for each Fund's time horizon, distribution requirements, and risk tolerance. NPO currently maintains [list Funds here, e.g., Operating Reserves, Endowments, Charitable Trust Funds, Annuity Reserves] and may add other Funds in the future. These policies apply to all NPO Funds, although the specific objectives, risk parameters, and asset allocation will vary, as appropriate, from Fund to Fund.

ASSET ALLOCATIONS

Actual asset allocations for each Fund will be established and maintained by NPO on the advice of its Consultant and/or Advisors, within the ranges provided in the following table:

	Cash	Fixed Income	Equities	Alternative Investments
Operating Reserves	0-100%	0-50%	n/a	n/a
Retirement Funds	0-25%	0-25%	25-50%	n/a
Endowments	0-10%	0-20%	25-75%	Up to 25% if approved by committe

When appropriate, specific objectives for each Fund, including specific asset allocation parameters and performance standards, may be reflected in an appendix attached to these policies. Such specific objectives shall nonetheless be within the foregoing ranges, which can only be modified by the Committee with the approval of the Board.

REBALANCING PROCEDURES

The Committee will monitor the asset allocation of each Fund based on reports provided by NPO's Consultant and/or Investment Advisors. The Committee may establish any reasonable rebalancing procedure based on either periodic reviews or departures from a range and may use its discretion to determine the timing of rebalancing actions. To achieve rebalancing, NPO may either move money from one asset class to another or may direct future contributions to and expenditures from particular classes as is most convenient.

INVESTMENT GUIDELINES

To accomplish its investment objectives, NPO is authorized to utilize any legal investment structure that holds publicly traded securities including separately managed portfolios, mutual funds, exchange traded funds, limited partnerships, and other commingled investment entities. This authority is subject to the requirements and restrictions contained in these policies.

When utilizing mutual funds or other commingled entities, the Committee shall see that NPO's staff, Consultant, and/or Investment Advisors have selected the investment entity appropriately based on the strategies and provisions contained in the entity's prospectus. In that event, the terms and conditions of the prospectus are deemed to control the entity's internal asset allocation, asset quality, diversification, and other requirements.

For purposes of these investment policies, all private (non–publicly traded) investments and all investments prohibited under the Risk-Based Restrictions, below, will be considered Alternative Investments. Alternative Investments may only be used with the approval of the Investment Committee granted in accordance with the exception processes described below.

INVESTMENT RESTRICTIONS

NPO's investment assets are to be managed with regard to the following restrictions for either tax, risk, or mission purposes:

Tax-Based Restrictions

NPO is a charitable organization under § 501(c)(3) of the Internal Revenue Code. Consequently, its income is generally exempt from federal and state income tax with the exception of income that constitutes Unrelated Business Taxable Income (UBTI). Since UBTI can be generated by leveraged investments (resulting in "debt-financed income"), NPO will not utilize margin, short selling, or other leveraged investment strategies unless the Investment Committee grants a specific exception as described below.

Risk-Based Restrictions

NPO will not engage in commodities transactions or option strategies (puts, calls, straddles) nor will it invest in any non–publicly traded securities including but not limited to managed futures funds, hedge funds, private equity funds, or other alternative investments unless approved by the Committee as provided below.

MISSION-BASED INVESTMENT CRITERIA

NPO desires to invest in companies whose business conduct is consistent with NPO's goals and beliefs. Therefore, NPO's Consultant and/or Investment Advisors will use their best efforts to avoid holding securities of any company known to participate in businesses the Board deems to be socially or morally inconsistent with NPO objectives. The Committee will provide Advisors with a statement of NPO's mission guidelines and restrictions.

EXCEPTIONS TO THE INVESTMENT RESTRICTIONS

The Board recognizes the evolving nature of the investment world and that, under some circumstances, NPO may wish to utilize newer or more complex investment strategies. Therefore, the Investment Committee is authorized to grant exceptions to the foregoing restrictions. For tax-based restrictions, the Committee is to determine if a particular strategy or investment will generate UBTI, for which it may rely on advice of counsel.

When granting exceptions to the Risk-Based restrictions or otherwise approving Alternative Investments, the Committee must determine that the potential rewards outweigh the incremental risks and the Committee, or the Committee's retained investment consultant, must complete the additional Alternative Investment Due Diligence described in the exhibit to these policies. All such exceptions shall be made in writing and shall be communicated to the Board as part of the next regular Investment Committee report.

PROXY VOTING

Subject to any specific instructions received from NPO or contained in NPO's mission guidelines (see Mission-Based Investment Criteria, above), each Advisor shall vote proxies according to their firm's established procedures and shall provide a copy of such procedures to the Committee upon request.

CUSTODY AND SECURITIES BROKERAGE

The Committee will establish such custodial and brokerage relationships as are necessary for the efficient management of NPO's Funds. Whenever the Committee has not designated a brokerage relationship, then NPO Investment Advisors may execute transactions wherever they can obtain best price and execution.

CASH FLOW REQUIREMENTS

NPO will be responsible for advising the Consultant and each Advisor in a timely manner of NPO's cash distribution requirements from any managed portfolio or Fund. Each Advisor is responsible for providing adequate liquidity to meet such distribution requirements.

REPORTING REQUIREMENTS

1) Monthly — The Committee will obtain written monthly custodial statements. Such statements should contain all pertinent transaction details for each account that holds all or a portion of any NPO investment Funds. Each monthly statement should include:

   a) the name and quantity of each security purchased or sold, with the price and transaction date; and,

   b) a description of each security holding as of month-end, including its percentage of the total portfolio, purchase date, quantity, average cost basis, current market value, unrealized gain or loss, and indicated annual income (yield) at market.

   In addition, if not included in the custodial reports, the Consultant and/or the Investment Advisor(s) should provide a report for each Fund or portfolio showing the month-end allocation of assets between equities, fixed-income securities, and cash. The monthly review of custodial statements may be delegated to NPO accounting staff.

2) Quarterly — The Committee should obtain from its Investment Consultant and/or Investment Advisors, a detailed review of NPO's investment performance for the preceding quarter and for longer trailing periods as appropriate. Such reports should be provided as to each Fund and as to NPO investment assets in the aggregate. As to each Fund, the Committee should establish with its Investment Consultant and/or Investment Advisors the specific criteria for monitoring each Fund's performance including the index or blend of indices that are appropriate for the objectives of each Fund and for the investment style or asset class of each portfolio within a Fund. The Committee shall meet with the Consultant to conduct such reviews to the extent it deems necessary.

3) Periodically — The Committee should meet with its Investment Consultant at least annually to review all aspects of NPO's investment assets. Such a review should include (1) strategic asset allocation, (2) manager and investment entity performance, (3) anticipated additions to or withdrawals from Funds, (4) future investment strategies, and (5) any other matters of interest to the Committee.

APPENDIX II

ALTERNATIVE INVESTMENT DUE DILIGENCE GUIDELINES

Please see the attached CD-ROM for a downloadable and customizable version of the following sample policies.

EXECUTIVE SUMMARY

Nonprofit Organization's (NPO's) Investment Policies reflect the prudent investor rules and generally restrict investments to portfolios of publicly traded stocks, bonds, and cash, either directly or through mutual funds or similar structures. Subject to appropriate, additional due diligence, NPO's policies also allow reasonable allocations to alternative investments which, for this purpose, means any investment that is not publicly traded or that would not otherwise satisfy NPO's investment guidelines.

DUE DILIGENCE REQUIREMENTS FOR ALTERNATIVE INVESTMENTS

For alternative investments, the NPO Investment Management Committee looks to the advisor making the recommendation to complete a reasonable level of due diligence and to provide the following information on each recommended alternative investment:

Risk-adjusted return enhancement

- Covariance analysis relative to the other assets in the portfolio
- Track record across market cycles
- Performance relative to comparable managers or strategies

Advisory firm due diligence

- Related parties/Conflicts of Interest
- Manager qualifications
- Aggregate fees

Investment Manager Documentation

- Private placement subscription documents
- Form ADV
- Financial statements
- LLC operating agreement
- Sample performance reports
- Analysis of tax issues (UBTI)

RELATIONSHIP OF INVESTMENTS TO GIFT ACCEPTANCE POLICIES

NPO has somewhat greater discretion in accepting gifts than it does in making investments. While the foregoing restrictions on nonconforming alternatives would still apply, NPO does not need to evaluate gifts of assets to be sold under prudent investor standards. Consequently, NPO routinely accepts a wide range of assets as gifts in addition to cash and publicly traded securities. Potentially acceptable gifts include real estate and other tangible assets, closely held stock, and interests in partnerships or other entities that hold alternative investments. NPO's Gift Acceptance Policies establish the rules for accepting such assets and are designed to ensure proper valuations, compliance with IRS standards for charitable deductions, and the ability of NPO to sell the gifted asset in a reasonable period of time.

NPO ALTERNATIVE INVESTMENT PROFILE FORM

The undersigned advisor ("Advisor") hereby recommends that the NPO Investment Management Committee consider an investment in

_____
(Name of Investment Offering)

in the amount of _____ dollars ($_____).

The offering is best described as a:

❏ Hedge Fund

❏ Fund of Hedge Funds

❏ Private Equity Fund

❏ Managed Futures Fund

❏ Annuities or other Insurance Products

❏ Structured Note

❏ Other (Describe) _____

RISK-ADJUSTED PERFORMANCE ANALYSIS

Based on our analysis of the investment and of the other assets in the portfolio, we believe the recommended allocation to this investment should enhance risk-adjusted returns across a full market cycle. A copy of the materials supporting our analysis is attached (e.g., Covariance analysis, manager performance analysis, risk-adjusted performance relative to comparable strategies and managers, Monte Carlo analysis).

NPO APPROVAL REQUIREMENTS

The recommended investment strategy:

- ❏ Permits withdrawals (Check all that apply)

  - ❏ Monthly

  - ❏ Quarterly

  - ❏ Annually

- ❏ The entity managing the investment is itself a registered investment advisor with audited financial statements and at least $10 million under management for the past three years.

- ❏ The investment structure will not generate unrelated business taxable income nor subject NPO to future capital calls or other additional mandatory contributions.

- ❏ The entity holding the recommended investment has an established procedure for reporting valuation at least annually (e.g., audit, publicly traded units, third-party appraisal) and the valuation procedure satisfies the auditing requirements that apply to NPO as a nonprofit investor.

- ❏ The donor will not receive any compensation from any investment advisor associated with the recommended investment and none of the investment advisors are related parties to the donor as that concept is defined in the Pension Protection Act of 2006.

- ❏ The Nonprofit Organization will not be listed as an investor in any materials that are used to sell or promote an investment in the recommended strategy, nor will the manager of the strategy use NPO's investment for marketing purposes or disclose to anyone that NPO is an investor in the strategy except to the extent required by state or federal regulations.

ADVISORY FIRM DUE DILIGENCE

Our firm has conducted due diligence on the offering and the promoters and managers of the offering and are satisfied that it is an appropriate investment for NPO. In that regard:

- The offering will not generate unrelated business taxable income as a result of the absence of leverage, an off-shore investment structure, or both.

- The manager has been in business since _____ (date) and currently has $_____ assets under management.

- The manager's audited financial statement are provided by _____ _____ (Name of Firm/Contact).

- Aggregate fees are: (describe) _____ _____ out of which our firm will receive _____.

- The attached documentation adequately describes the offering.

LIQUIDITY AND DISTRIBUTIONS

We have reviewed the liquidity and redemption provisions of the proposed investment with NCO's Chief Financial Officer who has advised us of the levels of anticipated distributions from the fund of which the proposed alternative investment would be a part. Based on the liquidity of the recommended investment and the remaining assets in the portfolio, the portfolio should be able to meet the intended distributions and meet a minimum 5 percent distribution for at least _____ years without liquidating the recommended investment.

APPENDIX III
SAMPLE SPENDING POLICY

Please see attached CD-ROM for a downloadable and customizable version of the following sample policy.

The Fund shall annually distribute an amount equal to 5 percent (5%) of the Fund's average value as calculated in this paragraph. The distributions shall be made quarterly in an amount equal to $1\frac{1}{4}$ percent (1.25%) of the calculated Distribution Value. The Distribution Value is the average of the fair market value of the Fund as of the close of each of the preceding 12 calendar quarters. The Fund's market value shall be based upon all assets in the Fund including principal and retained income, adjusted for all gains and losses, whether realized or unrealized, and determined as of the last business day of the quarter. The distributions shall be made promptly following the close of each quarter. To the extent that it may legally do so, the organization shall interpret this policy as satisfying a gift provision that calls for retaining principal and distributing income.

APPENDIX IV

UNIFORM PRUDENT MANAGEMENT OF INSTITUTIONAL FUNDS ACT

Please see the attached CD-ROM for an electronic copy of UPMIFA. Reprinted with permission from the National Conference of Commisioners on Uniform State Laws.

UNIFORM PRUDENT MANAGEMENT OF INSTITUTIONAL FUNDS ACT

drafted by the

NATIONAL CONFERENCE OF COMMISSIONERS ON UNIFORM STATE LAWS

and by it

APPROVED AND RECOMMENDED FOR ENACTMENT

IN ALL THE STATES

at its

ANNUAL CONFERENCE

MEETING IN ITS ONE-HUNDRED-AND-FIFTEENTH YEAR

HILTON HEAD, SOUTH CAROLINA

July 7-14, 2006

Copyright ©2006

By

NATIONAL CONFERENCE OF COMMISSIONERS ON UNIFORM STATE LAWS

Copies of the Act with drafting comments may be obtained from:

NATIONAL CONFERENCE OF COMMISSIONERS

ON UNIFORM STATE LAWS

211 E. Ontario Street, Suite 1300

Chicago, Illinois 60611

312/915-0195

www.nccusl.org

UNIFORM PRUDENT MANAGEMENT OF INSTITUTIONAL FUNDS ACT
TABLE OF CONTENTS

SECTION 1. SHORT TITLE. 82

SECTION 2. DEFINITIONS 82

SECTION 3. STANDARD OF CONDUCT IN MANAGING
AND INVESTING INSTITUTIONAL FUND 83

SECTION 4. APPROPRIATION FOR EXPENDITURE OR
ACCUMULATION OF ENDOWMENT FUND; RULES OF CONSTRUCTION . . . 86

SECTION 5. DELEGATION OF MANAGEMENT AND
INVESTMENT FUNCTIONS. 87

SECTION 6. RELEASE OR MODIFICATION OF RESTRICTIONS
ON MANAGEMENT, INVESTMENT, OR PURPOSE. 88

SECTION 7. REVIEWING COMPLIANCE 90

SECTION 8. APPLICATION TO EXISTING INSTITUTIONAL FUNDS 90

SECTION 9. RELATION TO ELECTRONIC SIGNATURES IN GLOBAL
AND NATIONAL COMMERCE ACT. 90

SECTION 10. UNIFORMITY OF APPLICATION AND CONSTRUCTION 90

SECTION 11. EFFECTIVE DATE 90

SECTION 12. REPEAL 90

UNIFORM PRUDENT MANAGEMENT OF INSTITUTIONAL FUNDS ACT

SECTION 1. SHORT TITLE. This [act] may be cited as the Uniform Prudent Management of Institutional Funds Act.

SECTION 2. DEFINITIONS. In this [act]:

> (1) "Charitable purpose" means the relief of poverty, the advancement of education or religion, the promotion of health, the promotion of a governmental purpose, or any other purpose the achievement of which is beneficial to the community.

> (2) "Endowment fund" means an institutional fund or part thereof that, under the terms of a gift instrument, is not wholly expendable by the institution on a current basis. The term does not include assets that an institution designates as an endowment fund for its own use.

(3) "Gift instrument" means a record or records, including an institutional solicitation, under which property is granted to, transferred to, or held by an institution as an institutional fund.

(4) "Institution" means:

>(A) a person, other than an individual, organized and operated exclusively for charitable purposes;

>(B) a government or governmental subdivision, agency, or instrumentality, to the extent that it holds funds exclusively for a charitable purpose; or

>(C) a trust that had both charitable and noncharitable interests, after all noncharitable interests have terminated.

(5) "Institutional fund" means a fund held by an institution exclusively for charitable purposes. The term does not include:

>(A) program-related assets;

>(B) a fund held for an institution by a trustee that is not an institution; or

>(C) a fund in which a beneficiary that is not an institution has an interest, other than an interest that could arise upon violation or failure of the purposes of the fund.

(6) "Person" means an individual, corporation, business trust, estate, trust, partnership, limited liability company, association, joint venture, public corporation, government or governmental subdivision, agency, or instrumentality, or any other legal or commercial entity.

(7) "Program-related asset" means an asset held by an institution primarily to accomplish a charitable purpose of the institution and not primarily for investment.

(8) "Record" means information that is inscribed on a tangible medium or that is stored in an electronic or other medium and is retrievable in perceivable form.

SECTION 3. STANDARD OF CONDUCT IN MANAGING AND INVESTING INSTITUTIONAL FUND.

(a) Subject to the intent of a donor expressed in a gift instrument, an institution, in managing and investing an institutional fund, shall consider the charitable purposes of the institution and the purposes of the institutional fund.

(b) In addition to complying with the duty of loyalty imposed by law other than this [act], each person responsible for managing and investing an institutional fund shall manage and invest the fund in good faith and with the care an ordinarily prudent person in a like position would exercise under similar circumstances.

(c) In managing and investing an institutional fund, an institution:

> (1) may incur only costs that are appropriate and reasonable in relation to the assets, the purposes of the institution, and the skills available to the institution; and

> (2) shall make a reasonable effort to verify facts relevant to the management and investment of the fund.

(d) An institution may pool two or more institutional funds for purposes of management and investment.

(e) Except as otherwise provided by a gift instrument, the following rules apply:

> (1) In managing and investing an institutional fund, the following factors, if relevant, must be considered:

>> (A) general economic conditions;

>> (B) the possible effect of inflation or deflation;

>> (C) the expected tax consequences, if any, of investment decisions or strategies;

>> (D) the role that each investment or course of action plays within the overall investment portfolio of the fund;

>> (E) the expected total return from income and the appreciation of investments;

>> (F) other resources of the institution;

>> (G) the needs of the institution and the fund to make distributions and to preserve capital; and

>> (H) an asset's special relationship or special value, if any, to the charitable purposes of the institution.

> (2) Management and investment decisions about an individual asset must be made not in isolation but rather in the context of the institutional fund's portfolio of investments as a whole and as a part of an overall investment strategy having risk and return objectives reasonably suited to the fund and to the institution.

> (3) Except as otherwise provided by law other than this [act], an institution may invest in any kind of property or type of investment consistent with this section.

(4) An institution shall diversify the investments of an institutional fund unless the institution reasonably determines that, because of special circumstances, the purposes of the fund are better served without diversification.

(5) Within a reasonable time after receiving property, an institution shall make and carry out decisions concerning the retention or disposition of the property or to rebalance a portfolio, in order to bring the institutional fund into compliance with the purposes, terms, and distribution requirements of the institution as necessary to meet other circumstances of the institution and the requirements of this [act].

(6) A person that has special skills or expertise, or is selected in reliance upon the person's representation that the person has special skills or expertise, has a duty to use those skills or that expertise in managing and investing institutional funds.

SECTION 4. APPROPRIATION FOR EXPENDITURE OR ACCUMULATION OF ENDOWMENT FUND; RULES OF CONSTRUCTION.

(a) Subject to the intent of a donor expressed in the gift instrument [and to subsection (d)], an institution may appropriate for expenditure or accumulate so much of an endowment fund as the institution determines is prudent for the uses, benefits, purposes, and duration for which the endowment fund is established. Unless stated otherwise in the gift instrument, the assets in an endowment fund are donor-restricted assets until appropriated for expenditure by the institution. In making a determination to appropriate or accumulate, the institution shall act in good faith, with the care that an ordinarily prudent person in a like position would exercise under similar circumstances, and shall consider, if relevant, the following factors:

(1) the duration and preservation of the endowment fund;

(2) the purposes of the institution and the endowment fund;

(3) general economic conditions;

(4) the possible effect of inflation or deflation;

(5) the expected total return from income and the appreciation of investments;

(6) other resources of the institution; and

(7) the investment policy of the institution.

(b) To limit the authority to appropriate for expenditure or accumulate under subsection (a), a gift instrument must specifically state the limitation.

(c) Terms in a gift instrument designating a gift as an endowment, or a direction or authorization in the gift instrument to use only "income", "interest", "dividends", or "rents, issues, or profits", or "to preserve the principal intact", or words of similar import:

> (1) create an endowment fund of permanent duration unless other language in the gift instrument limits the duration or purpose of the fund; and

> (2) do not otherwise limit the authority to appropriate for expenditure or accumulate under subsection (a).

[(d) The appropriation for expenditure in any year of an amount greater than seven percent of the fair market value of an endowment fund, calculated on the basis of market values determined at least quarterly and averaged over a period of not less than three years immediately preceding the year in which the appropriation for expenditure is made, creates a rebuttable presumption of imprudence. For an endowment fund in existence for fewer than three years, the fair market value of the endowment fund must be calculated for the period the endowment fund has been in existence. This subsection does not:

> (1) apply to an appropriation for expenditure permitted under law other than this [act] or by the gift instrument; or

> (2) create a presumption of prudence for an appropriation for expenditure of an amount less than or equal to seven percent of the fair market value of the endowment fund.]

SECTION 5. DELEGATION OF MANAGEMENT AND INVESTMENT FUNCTIONS.

(a) Subject to any specific limitation set forth in a gift instrument or in law other than this [act], an institution may delegate to an external agent the management and investment of an institutional fund to the extent that an institution could prudently delegate under the circumstances. An institution shall act in good faith, with the care that an ordinarily prudent person in a like position would exercise under similar circumstances, in:

> (1) selecting an agent;

> (2) establishing the scope and terms of the delegation, consistent with the purposes of the institution and the institutional fund; and

> (3) periodically reviewing the agent's actions in order to monitor the agent's performance and compliance with the scope and terms of the delegation.

(b) In performing a delegated function, an agent owes a duty to the institution to exercise reasonable care to comply with the scope and terms of the delegation.

(c) An institution that complies with subsection (a) is not liable for the decisions or actions of an agent to which the function was delegated.

(d) By accepting delegation of a management or investment function from an institution that is subject to the laws of this state, an agent submits to the jurisdiction of the courts of this state in all proceedings arising from or related to the delegation or the performance of the delegated function.

(e) An institution may delegate management and investment functions to its committees, officers, or employees as authorized by law of this state other than this [act].

SECTION 6. RELEASE OR MODIFICATION OF RESTRICTIONS ON MANAGEMENT, INVESTMENT, OR PURPOSE.

(a) If the donor consents in a record, an institution may release or modify, in whole or in part, a restriction contained in a gift instrument on the management, investment, or purpose of an institutional fund. A release or modification may not allow a fund to be used for a purpose other than a charitable purpose of the institution.

(b) The court, upon application of an institution, may modify a restriction contained in a gift instrument regarding the management or investment of an institutional fund if the restriction has become impracticable or wasteful, if it impairs the management or investment of the fund, or if, because of circumstances not anticipated by the donor, a modification of a restriction will further the purposes of the fund. The institution shall notify the [Attorney General] of the application, and the [Attorney General] must be given an opportunity to be heard. To the extent practicable, any modification must be made in accordance with the donor's probable intention.

(c) If a particular charitable purpose or a restriction contained in a gift instrument on the use of an institutional fund becomes unlawful, impracticable, impossible to achieve, or wasteful, the court, upon application of an institution, may modify the purpose of the fund or the restriction on the use of the fund in a manner consistent with the charitable purposes expressed in the gift instrument. The institution shall notify the [Attorney General] of the application, and the [Attorney General] must be given an opportunity to be heard.

(d) If an institution determines that a restriction contained in a gift instrument on the management, investment, or purpose of an institutional fund is unlawful, impracticable, impossible to achieve, or wasteful, the institution, [60 days] after notification to the [Attorney General], may release or modify the restriction, in whole or part, if:

(1) the institutional fund subject to the restriction has a total value of less than [$25,000];

(2) more than [20] years have elapsed since the fund was established; and

(3) the institution uses the property in a manner consistent with the charitable purposes expressed in the gift instrument.

SECTION 7. REVIEWING COMPLIANCE. Compliance with this [act] is determined in light of the facts and circumstances existing at the time a decision is made or action is taken, and not by hindsight.

SECTION 8. APPLICATION TO EXISTING INSTITUTIONAL FUNDS. This [act] applies to institutional funds existing on or established after [the effective date of this act]. As applied to institutional funds existing on [the effective date of this act] this [act] governs only decisions made or actions taken on or after that date.

SECTION 9. RELATION TO ELECTRONIC SIGNATURES IN GLOBAL AND NATIONAL COMMERCE ACT. This [act] modifies, limits, and supersedes the Electronic Signatures in Global and National Commerce Act, 15 U.S.C. Section 7001 et seq., but does not modify, limit, or supersede Section 101 of that act, 15 U.S.C. Section 7001(a), or authorize electronic delivery of any of the notices described in Section 103 of that act, 15 U.S.C. Section 7003(b).

SECTION 10. UNIFORMITY OF APPLICATION AND CONSTRUCTION. In applying and construing this uniform act, consideration must be given to the need to promote uniformity of the law with respect to its subject matter among states that enact it.

SECTION 11. EFFECTIVE DATE. This [act] takes effect . . . .

SECTION 12. REPEAL. The following acts and parts of acts are repealed:

(a) [The Uniform Management of Institutional Funds Act]

APPENDIX V
SELF-GUIDED INVESTMENT AUDIT

This self-assessment form is designed to allow input from multiple staff and committee members. Its questions address all of the issues that an investment consultant would normally consider in preparing an investment strategy. Completing the form will give your organization a very good handle on what you have to manage, your attitudes toward risk, and other factors. Please see the attached CD-ROM for a downloadable and customizable version of the following form.

Part I: General Information

(This portion is to be completed by the chief executive.)

1. Institution: _____

2. Senior Staff: Name   Phone

Chief Executive _____ _____

Senior Development
Officer _____ _____

Chief Financial
Officer _____ _____

Board Chair _____ _____

Investment Committee
Chair _____ _____

3. Type of Institution: School or College   Retirement Home

                              Hospital   Church

                              Pension Plan   Other Religious Organization

                              Public Foundation   Social Service Agency

                              Private Foundation   Other Public Charity

4. Business Structure: Unincorporated Nonprofit Association

   Nonprofit Corporation (Type) _____

   Limited Liability Company (Type)_____

   Other: _____

5. Mission Statement: *(Attach copy or brief narrative description.)*

6. Approximate Annual Budget:

$_____

(For reference purposes, please attach a copy of your most recent financial statements.)

7. Origins: Founded By: _____ Date:_____

Founded in (City, State, Country): _____

8. Incorporation: State: _____ Date:_____

9. Address of Corporate Headquarters:

_____

_____

_____

10. Geographic Service Area: *(Describe and list states in which you have at least one full-time employee and a physical location.)*

_____

_____

_____

Part II: Development (Fundraising) Information

(This portion is to be completed by the Senior Development Officer.)

1. Current Staffing of Development Program

Development Staff	Number	
Full-Time Professionals		
Full-Time Support Staff		
Other Staff (Names) who spend some time in Development	Regular position	% of Time Spent in Development

2. What percentage of your organization's total income comes from donations (gifts as opposed to fees for services, sales of products, etc.)?

_____

3. When did you start a full-time fundraising program?

_____

4. When did you start soliciting and/or accepting planned gifts?

_____

5. Please indicate the composition of gift income by category over the last three years.

	Average annual % in last 3 years	Highest annual % in last 3 years	Lowest annual % in last 3 years
Individual Contributions			
Corp. or Foundation Grants			
Bequests			
Lifetime Planned Gifts			
Special Events			
Gifts in Kind; Sponsorships			
Other:			

6. Of the categories listed in the above table, which do you believe are most likely to increase or decrease as a percentage of total annual gift income over the next three years?

Most likely to increase   _____   _____   _____

Most likely to decrease   _____   _____   _____

7. Please rank each of the following areas to indicate your fundraising priorities in terms of the allocation of development staff time for the coming year.

Fundraising Categories	Rank (1st–5th)	Allocable % of Staff Time
Current Annual Giving		
Planned (Deferred) Giving		
Capital Campaign		
Events; Sponsorships		
Corp/Foundation Grants		

8. What are the types, ages, and minimum dollar amounts of the deferred gifts and trusts that your organization accepts?

	Accepted (Y/N)	Minimum Age	Minimum $ Amount
Gift Annuities			
Charitable Remainder Trusts			
Charitable Lead Trusts			
Pooled Income Fund			
Donor-Advised Fund			
Life Interest Agreements in Real Property			
Other:			

9. Please briefly describe the additional staff support, funding, administrative support, or other assistance, if any, that you believe would permit you to more effectively raise funds for your organization over the next three years.

_____

_____

_____

_____

_____

10. Which of the following outside service providers do you currently use in development?

	Organization	Key Contact	First Service (Date)	Address (City, State)	Phone
Fundraising Consultants					
Collateral Material Services					
Securities Broker/Consultant					
Bank or Trust Company					
Investment Advisor					
CPA					
Attorney					
Insurance Agent or CFP					
Other:					

Part III: Investment Accounting, Gift Administration, and Reporting

(This portion is to be completed by the Chief Financial Officer.)

1. What planned gifts, endowments, or other funds does your organization currently have?

Type	No. of Gifts	Total Dollar	Median Size	Oldest Donor	Youngest Donor	Largest Gift – $	Smallest Gift – $
Gift Annuities							
Pooled Income Funds							
Remainder Trusts							
Revocable Trusts							
Operating Reserves							
Endowments							
Retirement Plans							
Capital Campaign Funds							
Other:							

2. How much do you spend administering planned gifts, endowments, or other reserves in each of the following categories: Accounting, Tax Returns, and Investment Management?

	$ Cost	Inside or Out	Service Provider or System Used
Gift Annuities			
Pooled Income Funds			
Remainder Trusts			
Revocable Trusts			
Operating Reserves			
Endowments			
Retirement Plans			
Capital Campaign Funds			
Other:			

3. How do you allocate administrative expenses for each of the following investment instruments (express on a percentage basis)?

	Operating Budget	Charged to Trust or Fund	Comments
Gift Annuities			
Pooled Income Funds			
Remainder Trusts			
Revocable Trusts			
Operating Reserves			
Endowments			
Retirement Plans			
Capital Campaign Funds			
Other:			

4. For each of the following instruments, how frequently do you make income distributions and send reports? Who serves as trustee on the trusts and what information do you provide when reporting?

Key: Frequency: Q = Quarterly, M = Monthly, A = Annual; Reports: 1099, K-1; IP (Investment Performance)

	Trustee	Distributions Frequency	Reports — Frequency and Content
Gift Annuities			
Pooled Income Funds			
Remainder Trusts			
Revocable Trusts			
Operating Reserves			
Endowments			
Retirement Plans			
Capital Campaign Funds			
Other:			

5. Do you have established investment policies for your managed funds? (Y/N).
   Who sets the policies? _____
   Are the policies disclosed to your donors? (Y/N)

6. Which outside service providers do you currently use in administering your
   planned gift and investment management assets?

	Organization	Key Contact	First Service (Date)	Address (City, State)	Phone
A) Securities Broker/ Consultant					
B) Bank or Trust Company					
C) Investment Advisor					
D) CPA					
E) Attorney					
F) Insurance Agent or CFP					
G) Other:					
H) Other:					

7. Who in your organization is responsible for supervising each of the following areas?

	Name	Phone
Trust Administration	_____	_____
Investment Management	_____	_____
Donor Reporting	_____	_____
Financial Accounting	_____	_____
Regulatory Compliance	_____	_____
Tax Compliance	_____	_____

8. Please indicate which of the service providers (listed in question 6), if any, assist you in the following areas. Write the letter for each provider (See #6) in the space provided.

- Communicating investment options to prospective donors? _____

- Establishing investment objectives and policies? _____

- Constructing planned giving presentations for major donors? _____

- Matching return expectations to spending needs and obligations? _____

- Reporting investment results to donors and management? _____

- Providing information for trustee decisions on risk/return relationships, asset allocation, and other similar issues? _____

- Analyzing investment performance for the benefit of donors and management? _____

- Segregating charitable remainder trust funds for independent management based on category of trust (e.g., income only, income only with make-up, 5%, 8%, etc.)? _____

9. Do you accept gifts of illiquid assets, such as real estate and collectibles? _____

10. Who helps with the management and/or liquidation of such assets?

_____

11. What are the most pressing problems that you face in the areas of trust administration, investment management, or planned gift administration?

_____

_____

Part IV: Investment Philosophy and Objectives

(To be answered by the investment committee of the board or by the full board if there is no committee. For those organizations that maintain multiple funds, these questions should be answered with regard to the endowment or other perpetual or long-term funds.)

Goals and Objectives

1. How would you categorize your overall investment objectives? Choose one.

   _____ Growth — maximum growth of capital with little or no income consideration

   _____ Growth with Income — primarily capital growth with some focus on income

   _____ Balanced — equal emphasis on capital growth and income

   _____ Income Oriented — primary emphasis on income

   _____ Capital Preservation — preserve original value regardless of income or growth

2. What average annual "absolute" rate of return, if any, (as opposed to a return "relative" to a market index) do you consider appropriate for long-term investments?

   _____ % per year   _____ % per year above inflation (CPI)

   _____ Prefer a relative standard

3. Relative to popular stock market indices (such as the S&P 500), rank your preferences for portfolio performance; 1 is your strongest preference and 5 is what you least prefer.

   _____ Outperform the market in UP market years.

   _____ Decline less than the market in DOWN market years.

   _____ Outperform the market on average over an extended period, without regard to individual years.

   _____ Match market performance over an extended period.

   _____ Ignore relative performance and focus solely on the absolute return goal(s) identified in question 2, above.

4. Please rank your preference for the following investment performance reporting options from 1 to 5, with 1 being your strongest preference.

   _____ Measuring current return or yield relative to required distributions

   _____ Comparing account returns to an "absolute" percent return target

   _____ "Relative" comparison (comparing the account returns to various market indices)

_____ Comparing to a "real" return (i.e., exceeds the inflation factor by X%)

_____ Using "absolute" and "relative" total return measures without regard to yield

5. Please describe any specific return requirements or performance reporting concerns that have not been addressed by the preceding questions.

_____

_____

_____

_____

Risk Questions

6. Please rank the following risks in the order of greatest concern (1 being the highest concern and 6 being the lowest).

_____ The failure to generate enough current income to cover required distributions

_____ The possibility of not achieving an intended rate of return

_____ Decreasing purchasing power due to inflation

_____ Wide swings in the value of our investments over three to five years

_____ A large drop in the value of any one or more investments, wholly apart from overall portfolio performance

_____ Other: (Please specify.) _____

7. What is the maximum percentage loss you could tolerate in your most aggressively invested portfolio over the following time frames?

_____ % per quarter   _____ % in any two-year period

_____ % per year   _____ Other: (Please describe.) _____

8. What is the maximum dollar loss you could tolerate in your most aggressively invested portfolio over the following time frames?

$ _____ per quarter $ _____ in any two-year period

$ _____ per year   _____ Other: (Please describe.) _____

9. Compared to a broad stock market index such as the S&P 500, how much fluctuation can you tolerate in the equity portion of your portfolio any given year?

_____ Much more fluctuation than the market

_____ Slightly more fluctuation than the market

_____ Approximately the same fluctuation as the market

_____ Slightly less fluctuation than the market

_____ Much less fluctuation that the market

10. Please describe any risk concerns that the preceding questions have not addressed.

_____

_____

_____

Investment Advisor Questions

11. Which statement best reflects your opinion as to how managers should implement your investment goals?

_____ We should establish overall objectives for the plan and allow the manager complete discretion regarding implementation;

_____ We should establish asset allocation parameters with the investment manager and then allow the manager discretion in selecting investments within those parameters; or,

_____ We should establish asset allocation parameters with the investment manager and then actively participate in and/or supervise the day-to-day selection of investments.

12. How do you feel about giving investment discretion to a third-party investment management firm? Choose one.

_____ Very comfortable   _____ Somewhat uncomfortable

_____ Somewhat comfortable   _____ Very uncomfortable

13. Select the statement that best describes how you currently make investment decisions.

_____ We collect and analyze the facts and make decisions on our own.

_____ Others advise us and we make decisions based on their advice.

_____ Our advisors make the decisions.

14. Please briefly list or describe those aspects of your current investment management process that are working well and those that you believe have problems or could be improved. (Examples include performance, performance reporting, asset allocation, etc.)

Working Well:

_____

_____

Concerns — May Need Improvement: _____

_____

_____

_____

_____

15. Which of the following outside service providers presently provide your
organization with investment management assistance?

	Organization	Key Contact	First Service (Date)	Address (City, State)	Phone
Securities Broker/Consultant					
Bank or Trust Company					
Investment Advisor					
CPA					
Attorney					
Insurance Agent or CFP					
Other:					
Other:					
Other:					

Part V: Fund Information

(To be completed by the Chief Financial Officer)

Please answer a set of questions for each fund identified in Part II of this questionnaire.

Name of Fund: _____ Type of Fund:_____

1. General Portfolio Objective: (Select one.)

   _____ Capital Preservation — the preservation of capital with returns exceeding risk-free investments. Accordingly, the risk level should be low with minimal price volatility.

   _____ Income — modest growth of capital with the generation of income as the primary objective.

   _____ Growth and Income — primarily oriented toward growth of principal with a minor emphasis on portfolio income. Investments could include equities, debt instruments, and cash or cash equivalents for diversification and risk management.

   _____ Growth — growth of capital. The portfolio will exhibit increased volatility while expecting to outperform equity indices over a market cycle.

   _____ Aggressive Growth — aggressive growth of capital is the primary objective. The portfolio may accept higher volatility associated with aggressive growth while expecting to outperform equity indices over a market cycle.

2. Investment time horizon most appropriate for this account: (Select one.)

   _____ 10 years or more

   _____ Five to 10 years

   _____ Three to five years

   _____ Less than three years

3. Target rates of return: 1 year: ___.___% 3 years: ___.___% 5 years: ___.___%

4. What is the current relative risk tolerance for this fund?

   _____ More fluctuation than the market

   _____ Approximately the same fluctuation as the market

   _____ Less fluctuation than the market

   _____ Relative performance measures are inappropriate for this fund

5. What is the maximum loss you could tolerate in this fund over the following time frames?

_____ % per quarter

_____ % per year

_____ % in any two-year period

6. Is the fund taxable? _____ yes _____ no

7. If the fund is taxable, what is the:

Income tax rate: _____._____%   Capital gains tax rate: _____._____%

8. Other information

Minimum required annual yield (Dividend and Interest):
$_____

Anticipated annual contributions: $_____

Anticipated annual withdrawals: $_____

9. Please list the existing assets and attach a current portfolio statement, if available.

Asset Class	Percent Allocated	Dollar Amount
Cash/Cash Equivalents (includes mutual funds)		
Equities (includes mutual funds)		
Bonds (includes mutual funds)		
Real Estate (includes mutual funds, REITs, etc.)		
Private Placements (includes personal business)		
Other Investments (includes mutual funds)		

10. Indicate the current asset allocation percentages and the permitted range if such targets exist. If a category is prohibited, indicate with a "0" maximum percentage. If a category is required, indicate by stating the same percentage for minimum and maximum.

Asset Class	Current	Minimum	Maximum
Cash/Cash Equivalents			
U.S. Stocks			
Foreign Equities			
U.S. Investment Grade Bonds			
Junk Bonds			
Foreign Bonds			
Real Estate (includes mutual funds, REITs, etc.)			
Private Placements (includes personal business)			
Other Investments (includes mutual funds)			

11. Please describe on an attached page the purpose of this fund, any special income or other requirements, any restrictions on investments, and any special reporting requirements.

GLOSSARY

Alternative Investments: these are usually complicated investment structures, not ordinary shares or bonds, often in partnership format, and usually sold as private placements as opposed to publicly registered securities.

Asset Allocation: the process of allocating investment funds to different asset classes. This is usually done as part of the process of creating a portfolio with certain expected risk and return characteristics.

Asset Class: any of a number of categories of assets. The broadest categories for investment purposes include cash, equities (stocks), bonds, real estate, and commodities.

Bond: a loan in which the borrower commits to pay interest either at regular intervals or at maturity, in addition to repaying the principal amount at a certain date.

Capital Gain: the excess by which proceeds from the sale of a capital asset exceed the cost basis.

Certificate of Deposit (CD): a receipt for a deposit of funds in a financial institution that permits the holder to receive interest plus the deposit at maturity.

Charitable Gift Annuities: annuities contracts with a charity under which the purchaser receives an income stream for life with the charity retaining the balance of the funds after the income stream ends.

Commercial Paper: a short-term unsecured promissory note issued by a finance company or a relatively large industrial firm. The notes ($25,000 minimum) are generally sold at a discount from face value with maturities ranging from 30 to 270 days.

Commodity: a generic, largely unprocessed good that can be processed and resold. Commodities traded in the financial markets for immediate or future delivery include grains, metals, and minerals.

Common Stock: a class of capital stock that has no preference to dividends or any distribution of assets. Common stock normally conveys voting rights and is often termed capital stock if it is the only class of stock that a firm has outstanding. Common stockholders are the residual owners of a corporation in that they have a claim to what remains after every other party has been paid. The value of their interest depends on the success of the firm.

Convertible Security: a security that, at the option of the holder, may be exchanged for another asset, generally a fixed number of shares of common stock. Convertible issues frequently are fixed-income securities such as debentures and preferred stock. Their prices are influenced by both changes in interest rates and the values of the asset into which they may be exchanged.

Corporate Bond: a bond issued by a corporation, as opposed to a bond issued by the U.S. Treasury or a municipality.

Custody: the service of holding financial assets for others. The service typically includes collecting dividends and interest, delivering securities and receiving cash on sales, transferring cash and receiving securities on purchases, and issuing monthly reports — in addition to the safe keeping of the assets.

Debt Instruments: securities representing borrowed funds that must be repaid. Examples of debt securities include bonds, certificates of deposit, commercial paper, and debentures.

Derivative Instrument: a financial instrument whose value is based on, and determined by, another security or benchmark such as a stock, bond, futures contract, or commodity. One common example is the separation of the interest payment of a mortgage-backed bond from its principal obligation.

Diversification: the process of reducing the risk associated with any one investment by acquiring a group of unrelated investment assets. Effective diversification requires assets on which returns, over time, are not directly related to any other asset in the total investment portfolio. A diversified securities portfolio generally includes 18 to 20 issues of firms that are not similarly affected by the same outside economic events.

Dividend: a share of a company's net profits distributed by the company to a class of its stockholders. The dividend is paid in a fixed amount for each share of stock held.

Dow Jones Industrial Average: an index maintained and reviewed by editors of the *Wall Street Journal,* the DJIA is not limited to traditionally defined industrial stocks but serves as a measure of the entire U.S. market. Its averages are unique in that they are price weighted rather than market capitalization weighted. Their component weightings are therefore affected only by changes in the stocks' prices, in contrast with other indexes' weightings that are affected by both price changes and changes in the number of shares outstanding. For the sake of continuity, composition changes are rare, and generally occur only after corporate acquisitions or other dramatic shifts in a component's core business.

Endowment: funds established for long-term institutional support from which the organization may typically spend only a limited amount in order to ensure the funds' perpetual existence.

Equity: stock — both common and preferred.

Exchange Traded Fund: a type of index mutual fund that issues shares, which trade on an exchange. Exchange traded funds (also called ETFs) have the advantages of index funds plus the daily liquidity of a publicly traded stock, but there are commission charges on purchases and sales. One example is shares issued by Barclay's Global Investors.

Fiduciary: a person or an organization that is entrusted with the property of another party, in whose best interests the fiduciary is expected to act when holding, investing, or otherwise utilizing that party's property. A board member is a fiduciary relative to the business and assets of the corporation.

FINRA: the Financial Industry Regulatory Authority, which is the nongovernmental regulator of all securities firms doing business in the United States. It was formed by the consolidation of the National Association of Securities Dealers and the enforcement functions of the New York Stock Exchange in 2007.

Fixed-income Security: a security, such as a bond or preferred stock, that pays a constant income each period. Price changes in a fixed-income security are caused primarily by changes in long-term interest rates.

Hedge Fund: refers to a broad class of investments that share the following characteristics: (1) they are created in partnership format, (2) they are unconstrained by diversification requirements, and (3) they are typically free to pursue strategies like short selling (the technique of borrowing shares and selling them in the expectation that the shares decline in value). Hedge funds frequently use leverage (usually borrowed funds) and are almost always sold as private placements.

Index Fund: a mutual fund that intentionally mirrors the holdings of a particular securities index such as the S&P 500. Such funds do not attempt to earn incremental returns by selecting securities. Consequently, they are less expensive to maintain and usually have lower turnover than traditional mutual funds.

Inflation: a general increase in the price level of goods and services, which reduces the purchasing power of the affected currency.

Intermediate-term Funds: funds expected to be available in one to five years. They may be invested in fixed-income instruments, such as corporate or government bonds, in maturities that are appropriate for the length of time the funds are available.

Investment Grade: a designation applied to a bond or other fixed-income investment indicating its suitability for purchase by institutions. Investment-grade designations are made by various rating agencies such as Moody's and Standard & Poor's (S&P), based on the credit worthiness and financial strength of the company issuing the debt. S&P investment grade ratings are AAA, AA, A, and BBB.

Junk Bond: a high-risk, high-yield debt security that, if rated at all, is graded less than BBB. These securities are most appropriate for risk-oriented investors.

Leverage: use of fixed costs (typically borrowed funds) in an attempt to increase the rate of return from an investment by allowing the purchase of larger positions. While leverage can operate to increase rates of return, it also increases the amount of risk inherent in an investment.

Liquidity: a position in cash or in assets easily convertible to cash.

Long-term Funds: funds that always include permanent endowments and may also include retirement assets, gift-annuity reserves, or other funds with a long-term purpose and time horizon.

Margin Account: a brokerage account that permits an investor to purchase securities on credit and to borrow on securities already in the account. Interest is charged on any borrowed funds, but only for the period of time that the loan is outstanding.

Market Value: the price at which a security currently can be sold.

Money Market Fund: an open-ended mutual fund that invests in short-term, highly liquid instruments such as Treasury bills, commercial paper, banker's acceptances, and negotiable certificates of deposit.

Moody's: a trademark for one of the companies that issues ratings denoting the relative investment quality of corporate and municipal bonds.

Mutual Fund: open-end funds that are not listed for trading on a stock exchange and are issued by companies that use their capital to invest in other companies. Mutual funds sell their own new shares to investors and buy back their old shares upon redemption. Capitalization is not fixed and normally shares are issued as people want them.

NASDAQ: NASDAQ (National Association of Securities Dealers Automated Quotation System) is a computerized data system run by the National Association of Securities Dealers to provide brokers with price quotations for securities traded over the counter. NASDAQ today is where many leading companies are traded, including Microsoft, MCI, and Northwest Airlines.

Noncorrelation: the potential for managed futures funds to perform when traditional markets, such as stocks and bonds, may experience difficulty, thus reducing risk of investment. The degree of noncorrelation of any given managed futures fund will vary — some of the investments should go up in value and others should go down, balancing out one's gains and losses.

Operating Reserves: any funds being held for general spending within the next 12 months.

Opportunity Cost: the cost of something in terms of an opportunity forgone, or the value of the next-highest-valued alternative use of that resource.

Portfolio Theory: the theory of selecting an optimal combination of assets such that the investor secures the highest possible return for a given level of risk or the least possible risk for a given level of return. Using portfolio theory, an investor assembles a group of assets on the basis of how the individual assets interact with one another. Thus, a security would be purchased not on the basis of how that security is expected to perform in isolation but rather on the basis of how that security can be expected to influence the risk and return of the investor's entire portfolio.

Preferred Stock: a security that shows ownership in a corporation and gives the holder a claim prior to the claim of common stockholders on earnings, and also generally on assets, in the event of liquidation. Most preferred stock issues pay a fixed dividend set at the time of issuance.

Principal: capital funds, such as the amount contributed to a trust; the repayment obligation (as opposed to the interest obligation) on a bond; or the amount initially invested in securities by an investor.

Private Placement: a legal way to sell securities to a limited group of purchasers without having to comply with the securities-law requirements associated with selling shares to the general public.

Return on Investment: a measure of the total return an investor is able to earn (income plus capital appreciation) expressed as a percentage of the amount of his or her investment. Return on investment is calculated by dividing total assets into net profits and may be calculated on either a before-tax or after-tax basis.

Risk: within the investment community, "risk" usually means the variability of returns from an investment. The greater the variability (i.e., of dividend fluctuation or of security price), the greater the risk. Since investors are generally averse to risk, investments with greater inherent risk must promise higher expected returns. In more common parlance, risk is the chance of a result that is less than you had expected.

Risk-free Asset: an asset that has, theoretically, no risk or volatility. Such assets might include treasury bills, money market instruments, and certificates of deposit (under $100,000).

Risk-free Rate of Return: the risk-free rate of return is either a rate at which you could lend money to a risk-free asset such as a Treasury bill, or a rate at which you can actually borrow money. The most common measure of so-called risk-free return is the 30-day U.S. Treasury bill.

Sector: a group of securities that share certain common characteristics based, generally, on the type of products or services they provide. One common division allocates companies into the following sectors: Basic Materials, Consumer Cyclical, Consumer Non-Cyclical, Energy, Financial Services, Industrial, Technology, and Utilities.

Short Selling: selling a security that must be borrowed to make delivery. Short selling normally entails the sale of securities that are not owned by the seller in anticipation of profiting from a decline in the price of the securities.

Short-term Funds: those that might be spent within 12 months and generally should be kept in cash or cash equivalents, such as money market funds.

Specific Risk: the risk that any one stock can significantly diminish the portfolio's value.

Speculation: the taking of above-average risks to achieve above-average returns, generally during a relatively short period of time.

Standard & Poor's Corporation: an investment advisory service that publishes financial data. A subsidiary of McGraw-Hill, the company also rates debt securities and distributes a series of widely followed stock indices.

Standard & Poor's 500 Stock Index (S&P 500): an inclusive index made up of 500 stock prices including 400 industrials, 40 utilities, 20 transportation, and 40 financial issues. The Index is constructed using market weights (stock price times shares outstanding) to provide a broad indicator of stock price movements.

Time Horizon: the time interval over which an investment program is to be completed. An investor's time horizon is very important in determining the types of investments that should be selected.

Total Return: dividend or interest income plus any capital gain less capital losses and expenses. Total return is generally considered a better measure of an investment's return than dividends or interest alone.

United States Government Securities: all bonds issued by the U.S. Treasury or other agencies of the U.S. government.

United States Treasury bills: interest-bearing government notes with a term of one year or less and a minimum investment of $10,000.

Unrealized Gain: the increased market value of an asset that is still being held, compared with the asset's cost of acquisition.

Unrealized Loss: the reduction in value of an asset that is being held compared with the original cost.

Yield: the percentage return on an investment from dividends or interest.

SUGGESTED RESOURCES

The list of additional resources is divided into three categories as an aid to readers. First is a brief list of news services and Web sites that I actually look at on a regular basis. There's no particular magic to our selections but readers may find our list helpful.

Second is a list of General Resources that cover a number of topics discussed throughout the book.

Finally, we included a short section that lists sources of information on the Bernie Madoff and New Era scandals.

NEWS SERVICES AND WEB SITES

Financial Times. The *Financial Times* is the British equivalent of the *Wall Street Journal* and the only newspaper to which I currently subscribe. Basically, I read it every morning at Starbucks and thereby keep a finger on the financial pulse of the world. I prefer it to the *Wall Street Journal* for its less U.S.-centric world view. It's available by subscription in the U.S. See, also, www.FT.com

Agora Financial is the publisher of numerous subscription newsletters and of several free newsletters including *The Rude Awakening*, which is edited by my brother, Eric Fry. Both *Rude* and the *5 Min Forecast* are enjoyable and insightful, everyday reading. www.agorafinancial.com

Jim Grant, publisher of *Grant's Interest Rate Observer*, www.grantspub.com

Brian Wesbury, Chief Economist, First Trust Portfolios, www.ftportfolios.com/Retail/Research/EconomicResearch.aspx

Ray Dalio, Bridgewater Associates, *Daily Observations,* www.bwater.com/home/strategies--research/bridgewater-daily-observations.aspx

Paul Kasriel, director of economic research for Northern Trust, www.northerntrust.com

Nassim Taleb, www.fooledbyrandomness.com

GENERAL RESOURCES

Berger, Steven. *Understanding Nonprofit Financial Statements, Third Edition.* Washington, DC: BoardSource, 2008.

The third edition of this best-selling title has been thoroughly updated to reflect changes in financial practices and rules. It has been expanded to include practical tips for board members and a comprehensive glossary. It also includes a CD-ROM with a ready-made presentation designed to help your entire board understand and review the organization's finances.

Bernstein, Richard. *Navigate the Noise.* Hoboken, NJ: John Wiley & Sons, 2001.

Written by a top Wall Street analyst, this resource provides an interesting analysis of the problem with too much information in the modern investment world.

Bonner, William. *Financial Reckoning Day.* Hoboken, NJ: John Wiley & Sons, 2003.

It is helpful to listen to contrarians and, especially, those who have legitimate concerns that everything is not coming up roses. Bill Bonner is the president of Agora Publishing and the creator of *The Daily Reckoning*, a widely read contrarian's Internet newsletter, cited in "News Services and Web Sites" on page 115.

Cary, William L., and Craig B. Bright. *The Law and Lore of Endowment Funds.* New York: The Ford Foundation, 1969.

Cary, William L., and Craig B. Bright. *The Developing Law of Endowment Funds: The Law and the Lore Revisited.* New York: The Ford Foundation, 1974.

These two resources are the seminal studies whose conclusions and recommendations led to the adoption of the prudent investor rule. While technically dated, the thoughts and observations are still interesting and valuable.

Cohen, Jerome, Arthur Zeikel, and Edward D. Zinbarg. *Investment Analysis and Portfolio Management.* Burr Ridge, IL: Irwin, 1987.

This resource is one of the standard textbooks on modern portfolio theory. It is a good single volume for those who would like to dig deeper into investment management.

Commonfund Commentary

The Uniform Prudent Management Act proposes major changes in investment standards for nonprofits. Commonfund explains the latest changes to the standards for the management, investment, and expenditure of the endowment funds of nonprofit institutions known as the Uniform Prudent Management of Institutional Funds Act, or UPMIFA. www.commonfund.org/Commonfund/Archive/CIO+Commentary/UPMIFA_commentary.htm

Downes, John and Jordan Elliot Goodman. *Barron's Finance & Investment Handbook (6th ed.)*. Hauppage, NY: Barron's Educational Series, Inc., 2003.

This book, useful for both the novice and the more advanced investor, provides a thorough overview of almost every type of investment (including bonds, annuities, life insurance, etc.) and a comprehensive glossary of investment terms. It is handy when it comes to looking up unfamiliar terms and also contains an extensive listing (with contact information) of brokerages, banks, state and federal regulators, major publications, and Web sites.

Ellis, Charles. *Winning the Loser's Game (4th ed.)*. New York: McGraw-Hill, 2002.

This resource is an excellent little book by a well-known, well-respected investment consultant on the importance of fundamental policy decisions. For those wishing deeper insights from a policy and supervisory perspective, this is a must read.

Fi360, "Self-Assessment of Fiduciary Excellence (SAFE) for Investment Stewards" www.fi360.com/main/pdf/SAFE_steward.pdf. An assessment tool that assists (1) an investment steward in analyzing how well their organization meets a defined global fiduciary standard of excellence; and (2) investment stewards in improving their long-term investment performance.

F.B. Heron Foundation. *Handbook on Responsible Investment Across Asset Classes*. 2008, Boston College Center for Corporate Citizenship.

This guidebook contains a recent discussion of socially responsible investing. For additional information, see www.fbheron.org

Fry, Robert P. Jr., *Nonprofit Investment Policies: Practical Steps for Growing Charitable Funds*. Hoboken, NJ: John Wiley & Sons, 1998.

This book is essentially the "consultants' version" of *Who's Minding the Money?* It addresses the same subjects, focusing specifically on the development of investment policies for nonprofit organizations, but in considerably greater detail. Its purpose is to help those board members, executives, and consultants who are involved in supervising investment policies to approach that task with a greater understanding of the underlying rules and concepts. See also, "Finance & Investments," at www.wiley.com for an interesting selection of books on investing.

Hutten, Tim. *The New Fiduciary Standard: The 27 Prudent Investment Practices for Financial Advisers, Trustees, and Plan Sponsors*. Princeton, NJ: Bloomberg Press, 2005.

This book identifies the 27 prudent practices, organized under Five Steps, that were developed by the Foundation for Fiduciary Studies. The most far-reaching trend in the financial advisory business today is the move toward a fiduciary advisory standard of care. This book establishes for the industry a credible investment-decision process that will meet the growing expectations of investors and regulators for integrity, transparency, and disclosure of fees and conflicts that affect their returns.

Kurtz, Daniel L., and Sarah E. Paul. *Managing Conflicts of Interest: A Primer for Nonprofit Boards, Second Edition.* Washington, DC: BoardSource, 2006.

The key for nonprofit boards is not to try to avoid all possible conflict-of-interest situations, but to identify and follow a process for handling them effectively. How an organization manages conflicts of interest and ensures open and honest deliberation affects all aspects of its operations and is critical to making good decisions, avoiding legal problems and public scandals, and remaining focused on the organization's mission. *Managing Conflicts of Interest: A Primer for Nonprofit Boards* acknowledges the difficulty in identifying problematic conflicts of interest, and gives recommendations for practice.

Lang, Andrew. *Financial Responsibilities of Nonprofit Boards, Second Edition.* Washington, DC: Boardsource, 2009.

While nonprofit success is measured in more than just dollars, board members must maintain a close eye on the financial direction of the organization and its economic stability if they are to truly fulfill their fiduciary responsibility. This book uses nontechnical language to help board members gain a basic understanding of their financial oversight responsibilities and gives them a starting point for comprehending key financial data.

Lawrence, Barbara and Outi Flynn. *The Nonprofit Policy Sampler, Second Edition.* Washington, DC: BoardSource, 2006.

This tool provides key elements and practical tips for 48 topic areas, including investment policies, that are important for all nonprofit boards to address. Each topic includes anywhere from two to 10 sample documents so that nonprofit leaders can select an appropriate sample from which to start drafting or revising their own policy. All samples are professionally and legally reviewed.

Mackay, Charles. *Extraordinary Popular Delusions and the Madness of Crowds.* Hampshire, Great Britain; Harriman House LTD, 2003.

First published in 1841 under the title, *Memoirs of Extraordinary Popular Delusions,* this book is often referred to as one of the best discussions of market psychology ever written.

Malkiel, Burton. *A Random Walk Down Wall Street (9th Ed)*. New York: W.W. Norton and Company, 2007.

Using the dot-com crash as an object lesson in how not to manage your portfolio, this book offers a gimmick-free and vastly informative guide to navigating the turbulence of the market and managing investments with confidence. With its life-cycle guide to investing, it matches the needs of investors at any age bracket, presenting a fair overview of traditional approaches to investing that are a proven success.

McLaughlin, Thomas A. *Financial Committees*. Washington, DC: BoardSource, 2004.

Accountability is increasingly important to nonprofits, and every board must be engaged in understanding its fiduciary duties. Learn about the core responsibilities finance, audit, and investment committees can hold. Discover how these committees can address challenges in helping the rest of the board understand complicated fiscal issues. This book will also help finance committees to stress the importance of board member independence in oversight and audit functions, and prepare the board to address potential new legal regulations.

McLaughlin, Thomas A. "Financial Paradox." *The Nonprofit Times,* March 1, 2009.

Tom McLaughlin asks pertinent questions during a financial crisis. He focuses on liquidity, benefits from unrealized losses, cutting costs, freezing or postponing activities, lines of credit, and controlling your largest asset.

Miller, Clara. "Truth or Consequences: The Implications of Financial Decisions." *The Nonprofit Quarterly,* Summer 2008.

The author poses a question: Does diversifying revenue base improve financial health? The analysis indicates that some level of funding diversity is good, but overdoing it may increase costs and complicate operations, which can in turn decrease profitability.

Unlocking Profit Potential: Your Organization's Guide to Social Entrepreneurship. E-book. Washington, DC: BoardSource and Community Wealth Ventures, 2002. www.boardsource.org/Knowledge.asp?ID=2.1153

Discover how to take a proactive approach to generating revenue through social entrepreneurship, conducting profitable enterprises to support the organization's ability to fulfill its mission. This resource discusses concepts of social entrepreneurship, available options, key issues, the role of board members, and guidelines for determining the best business venture for the organization.

INFORMATION ON MADOFF AND NEW ERA SCANDALS

The New Era for Philanthropy Scandal is accurately discussed on Wikipedia.

http://en.wikipedia.org/wiki/New_Era_Philanthropy

The Madoff Scandal is discussed in many places in the press and online. The most interesting view, however, revolves around Harry Markopolos, who detailed the many reasons why the Madoff Hedge Fund looked like a Ponzi scheme in a report he sent to the SEC in 1999. An introduction to Markopolos and his efforts can be found at Wikipedia, http://en.wikipedia.org/wiki/Harry_Markopolos, and a copy of his report is available from the *Wall Street Journal* in the following online archive: http://online.wsj.com/documents/Madoff_SECdocs_20081217.pdf

DEDICATION

For my Dad — Who started teaching me about investing when I was 10.

ACKNOWLEDGMENTS

The biggest challenge in writing a book, is not finding enough to say but having enough friends to help you say it. I have been blessed over the years with many friends and colleagues who have helped me say things and, importantly, not say things! The very earliest version of this book was privately published by my then-employer, Van Deventer & Hoch, in 1996, and I have previously acknowledged those who helped with that and subsequent versions. So without naming names, thank you all once again.

For this effort, my brother, Eric, with whom I also work was particularly important. Over the years I have enjoyed introducing Eric as "the person who actually knows things about investing," as there is more than a modicum of truth in that statement. From his current work as the editor of *The Rude Awakening* and his former work as a hedge fund manager, Eric is intimately familiar with the workings of Wall Street without being caught up in its culture. Rather, from his home and office here in Laguna Beach, he works to help everyday people navigate the financial markets. His work in reading and commenting on this book was invaluable and helped me avoid numerous mistakes.

I also appreciate several friends who read and commented on the text including, Dave Johnson, the chief financial officer at the National Christian Foundation, Hilaire Atlee of Bullfrog Research LLC, Dana Pancrazi of the F.B. Heron Foundation, and Steve Chapman and Dave Worland, also of the National Christian Foundation. Danielle Henry, my editor at BoardSource, set an impossible deadline but then worked tirelessly to help us meet it.

Finally, thanks again to my wonderful wife, Susan, who cheerfully put up with me while I complained about the added work of writing a book, even though she had previously asked, "Are you sure you want to do that?"

Thank you all.

Bob Fry
Laguna Beach, California

ABOUT THE AUTHOR

Bob Fry is the chief investment advisor to the National Christian Foundation in Atlanta, Georgia, and the founding member of Makarios Investment Advisors in Laguna Beach, California. Immediately prior to forming Makarios, Bob worked for 10 years at Merrill Lynch in a number of investment and management positions. He served as Merrill Lynch Trust Company's first director of investments, in which capacity he supervised the investment processes on $10 billion of trust assets, was a member of the Merrill Lynch Trust Company board of directors, and was chairman of the Investment Committee.

Prior to joining Merrill Lynch, Bob was director of charitable services for Van Deventer & Hoch, Investment Counsel. While there, he assisted charitable organizations as a portfolio manager and consultant on the investment aspects of endowments and planned gifts. He also spent more than 10 years in private practice as a business and securities law attorney.

Bob earned a Bachelor of Arts degree from the University of Southern California and the degree of Juris Doctor from the University of California at Los Angeles. He is involved in a number of community organizations and is also a frequent seminar speaker at national events including the AICPA Not for Profit Conference and the Investment Management Consultants Association (IMCA). He is the author of *Nonprofit Investment Policies: Practical Steps for Growing Charitable Funds* (John Wiley & Sons, Hoboken, NJ, 1998).

Bob lives in Irvine, California, with his wife, Susan, a special education teacher, and their daughter Jennifer who is attending Chapman University School of Law. Bob and Susan have two other children, Katie, who is in medical school at Upstate Medical University, in Syracuse, New York, and Jonathan, a recent graduate of Baylor University in Waco, Texas, who now lives and works in Dallas, Texas.

Unlike many men over age 50, Bob has pretty much given up golf in favor of full-court pickup basketball where his friends often observe, "He can't shoot, but at least he's slow."

Bob is happy to respond to questions or comments and can be reached by e-mail at rfryjr@makariosllc.com.